Prisoners Their Own Warders

A Record of the Convict Prison at Singapore in the
Straits Settlements Established 1825

W. D. Bayliss, John Frederick Adolphus McNair

Alpha Editions

This edition published in 2024

ISBN 9789362519979

Design and Setting By
Alpha Editions
www.alphaedis.com
Email - info@alphaedis.com

Contents

Preface   - 1 -

Chapter I   - 5 -

Chapter II   - 12 -

Chapter III   - 20 -

Chapter IV   - 27 -

Chapter V   - 36 -

Chapter VI   - 42 -

Chapter VII   - 52 -

Chapter   - 58 -

Chapter IX   - 70 -

CATHEDRAL   - 72 -

GOVERNMENT HOUSE   - 74 -

INDUSTRIES   - 76 -

STONE QUARRYING   - 81 -

Chapter X

Chapter XI

Chapter XII DISEASES AND MALINGERING   - 102 -

Chapter XIII CONCLUSION   - 107 -

Preface

Some explanation appears to be due from us for writing this account of the Singapore Convict Jail so long after the date of its final abolition.

The truth is, that for several years it has been our opinion that it ought to be written by some one, and the same suggestion had often been made to one of us by the late Doctor Mouat, Inspector General of Jails, Bengal, and others who were well acquainted with its administration.

An opportunity lately occurred to bring us into communication on the subject, and when we came to compare the voluminous notes that each of us had collected during the time that the jail was in full vigour, we arrived at the conclusion that there was abundant material for a work upon it. It also appeared to us that there were some exceptional features in the training and discipline of these native convicts, that might even at this day prove of service to other Superintendents of native jails in different parts of India and the Colonies; while, at the same time, such a work would not be devoid of some interest to those who make a study of the punishment and reformation of the criminal class of all countries, a subject in regard to which, in spite of the great progress we have made, the last word has certainly not yet been said.

This, then, is our apology for the attempt we have made, and we trust that our joint labours may be received with indulgence.

When this old Singapore jail was put an end to in 1873, some six years after the transfer of the Straits Settlements to the Crown, the convicts then under confinement were removed to the Andaman Islands, at that time not long established as a penal settlement for India; while those on a ticket-of-leave were permitted to merge into the population, continuing to earn their livelihood as artizans, cow keepers, cart drivers, and the like. Those who were old and infirm were retained at Singapore at the expense of the Indian Government, and a certain number of convicts from Hongkong were returned to that colony to complete their sentences. There remained, therefore, only the local prisoners to be dealt with, and for these, under the subsequent orders of the Colonial Government, was planned and constructed by our Department, and under our supervision, a spacious prison on the cellular system, and situated on a more healthy site than the old convict jail, which had become surrounded by the buildings of the town.

We should much like to have given a consecutive history of this old jail from the date of its first construction until it was finally abolished, but unfortunately the jail registers have not been carefully kept from the beginning, or are not forthcoming; but we have had access to some old scattered letters and papers, and to statistics from the year 1844, since which time the records have been regularly kept from year to year.

A good deal of useful information has also come within our reach from works written upon Singapore and the Straits Settlements, and especially are we indebted to an *Anecdotal History of Singapore*, published by the *Free Press*, and extending from the year 1822 to 1856, which gives an interesting account of our early occupation of that island, and of the use to which the labour of these convicts was turned.

From the Memoirs of *Sir Stamford Raffles*, written by his widow in 1830, and from his *Life* by Demetrius Charles Boulger, in 1897, we have been able to trace that, so far back as the year 1823, there were between 800 and 900 of these Indian convicts at our settlement of Bencoolen, on the south-west coast of Sumatra; and that, when this place was conceded to the Dutch by the London treaty of 1825, these convicts were removed to Penang, and were subsequently distributed amongst the three settlements of Penang, Malacca, and Singapore. This distribution would in all probability have taken place about the year 1825, when Singapore was incorporated with Penang and Malacca, under the Governor and Council of the Incorporated Settlements.

We think the account which we are about to give of the various employments of these Indian convicts at Singapore, will abundantly show how considerably this important settlement has benefited by their early introduction. They made most of the roads in the settlement, including timber bridges, viaducts and tunnels, and executed for the Government many important public buildings. Moreover, when released from imprisonment upon a ticket-of-leave, they were absorbed innoxiously into the native community, and again contributed to the advantage of the place in the various occupations they had recourse to, in order to obtain an honest livelihood. By a judicious system of rewards, and a graduated scale of promotion, a very remarkable spirit of industry was infused into the bulk of these convicts during their incarceration, and it may be honestly said that this was effected without the sacrifice of that wholesome discipline always essential in the control especially of the criminal class.

We could not, of course, interfere with their religion, but by a well-judged scale of punishments and rewards, and by instruction given to them in their own vernacular, we endeavoured to raise their character by helping them to good conduct, and to a better way of living. To encourage and foster that industry to which we have referred, we taught them the trades to which each of them appeared to be best adapted, and held out to them the hope that they might again become good citizens, and earn for themselves a creditable subsistence; and, as it was our practice to deal with each of them "individually," we were often made aware that there was many an honest heart immured within those prison walls.

In the narrative we have given of the Settlements, it may seem that we have dwelt at too great length upon their early history, but we thought it would add to the interest of the work, if we gave what is really only a limited sketch of the various places to which those Indian convicts were first banished beyond the seas.

In the initiation of the system of industrial training among these convicts, special credit is due to the late General (then Captain) Man, who in his early years had been trained at Chatham as a sapper. The late Colonel Macpherson, who succeeded him, carried on and improved the system, and both these officers were well seconded in their efforts by the late Mr. J. Bennett, C.E., who practically was their clerk of the works. Mr. Bennett subsequently rose to a high position in the Department.

It would be impossible to mention the names of all the subordinate staff, but Burnett, Stuart, and Lamb are prominent in our recollection as having done good service as warders and instructors.

In 1864, the Resident of Rhio, Java, Mr. E. Netscher, was appointed by the Dutch Government to study and report upon the convict system in force in Singapore, and both the Siam and Japan Governments sent special missions for the like purpose, the mission from Japan being accompanied by Mr. Hall, of the British Consulate. Many others, also, recorded their opinions in its favour, and some among them were authorities upon prison systems pursued in some parts of both Europe and America.

The local government, we should add, in their direction of this convict establishment, fully recognised that the distinctive feature in the native mind was to look to one rather than to many masters, to one European executive officer rather than to a collective body of magistrates, and, therefore, beyond that general supervision which the Government must ever assume over its Departments, it committed the whole of the management, discipline, and control of this large body of convicts entirely to their Superintendent, under the approved rules and regulations for his guidance, and for the administration of the whole establishment.

J. F. A. McNAIR, R.A., C.M.G.

W. D. BAYLISS.

Plate I.

Chapter I

EARLY RECORDS OF BENCOOLEN AND OBSERVATIONS ABOUT CONVICTS

In opening this account of the old convict jail at Singapore, it will be necessary to refer, as we have said, in some little detail to the history of the settlements of Bencoolen, Penang, and Malacca, to which convicts from India were first sent, prior to their reception into the Singapore prison.

The first penal settlement was Bencoolen, the Banka-Ulu of the Malays, to which they were transported from India about the year 1787, much about the same time that transportation to Australia for English convicts was sanctioned by our laws.

Bencoolen was singularly adapted as a receptacle for convict labour; it was not a populous place when we took it in 1685, nor, as far as we can gather, had the population much increased up to the year 1787, and the few Sumatrans and Malays that were its inhabitants were an indolent race, and preferred a life of ease to any kind of labour. They were content to get their livelihood from fishing, and they had no artificial wants. They would occasionally work upon pepper plantations, and would bring the berries to Bencoolen for sale to British merchants. Labour was therefore wanted here, and the East India Company thought that by its introduction they would make of Bencoolen a thriving settlement; but as it turned out they were greatly disappointed, for both pepper and camphor, which were the only commodities there for trade, greatly declined; and commerce, which was all-important to the East India Company, almost entirely disappeared after its establishment for some few years. It was a miserable place from all accounts, and was described by Captain James Lowe, in 1836, "as an expensive port, and of no use to any nation that might possess it," and he only echoed what was previously said of it by William Dampier, who had once been there in the humble position of a gunner, that it was "a sorry place, sorrily governed, and very unhealthy." So unhealthy was it, that it became necessary as early as 1714 to remove the Residency and offices to a point of land about two miles further off the coast, which was called Fort Marlborough; but even this locality was found not to be beyond the reach of malaria, and the place continued, as Crawfurd says, to be more or less unhealthy down to the cession of the settlement in 1825. But it had, however, done its work in providing for us a firm footing in those seas, and was a help to the next step in our progress towards a wider empire.

It is important to relate here that its last Lieut.-Governor was the founder of our now important settlement of Singapore. He took up the appointment at Bencoolen on the 20th March, 1818, founded Singapore in 1819, returned to Bencoolen in 1820, and finally left for England in 1824.

It is not our present purpose to dwell upon the intellectual and moral greatness of this remarkable man, for full justice has been done to his memory in the recent account of his life by Demetrius Boulger, and by an impressive tribute to his worth by General Sir Andrew Clarke, R.E., G.C.M.G., in a paper read by him in May last at the Royal Institution.

It is of course impossible at this late date to trace what was done in connection with the convicts on their first arrival at this settlement, though we gather from old letters that they were employed principally upon road-making, and on clearing estates which, "owing to their owners having died intestate, had reverted to the State." They were also let out to planters on a guarantee as to their not quitting the settlement.

The first authentic information we have in regard to the management and treatment of these convicts is from a letter to the Government by Sir Stamford Raffles, written from Bencoolen in 1818; which we give bodily from his Life, written by his widow in 1830. It is a paper which gives evidence of the soundness of his views upon this subject, and indeed it may be truly said, that with every question with which he had to deal he always displayed the greatest judgment and keenness of insight.

It is as follows:—

"But there is another class of people that call for immediate consideration. Since 1787 a number of persons have been transported to this place from Bengal for various crimes of which they have been found guilty.

The object of the punishment as far as it affects the parties must be the reclaiming them from their bad habits, but I much question whether the practice hitherto pursued has been productive of that effect. This I apprehend to be, in a great measure, in consequence of sufficient discrimination and encouragement not having been shown in favour of those most inclined to amendment, and perhaps to the want of a discretionary power in the chief authority to remit a portion of the punishment and disgrace which is at present the common lot of all. It frequently happens that men of notoriously bad conduct are liberated at the expiration of a limited period of transportation, whilst others, whose general conduct is perhaps unexceptional, are doomed to servitude till the end of their lives.

As coercive measures are not likely to be attended with success, I conceive that some advantage would arise from affording inducements to good conduct by holding out the prospect of again becoming useful members of society, and freeing themselves from the disabilities under which they labour. There are at present about 500 of these unfortunate people. However just the original sentence may have been, the crimes and characters of so numerous a body must necessarily be very unequal, and it is desirable that some discrimination should be exerted in favour of those who show the disposition to redeem their character. I would suggest the propriety of the chief authority being vested with a discretionary power of freeing such men as conduct themselves well from the obligation of service, and permitting them to settle in the place and resume the privileges of citizenship. The prospect of recovering their characters, of freeing themselves from their present disabilities, and the privileges of employing their industry for their own advantage would become an object of ambition, and supply a stimulus to exertion and good conduct which is at present wanting.

It rarely happens that any of those transported have any desire to leave the country; they form connections in the place, and find so many inducements to remain, that to be sent away is considered by most a severe punishment.

While a convict remains unmarried and kept to daily labour very little confidence can be placed in him, and his services are rendered with so much tardiness and dissatisfaction that they are of little or no value; but he no sooner marries and forms a small settlement than he becomes a kind of colonist, and if allowed to follow his inclinations he seldom feels inclined to return to his native country.

I propose to divide them into three classes. The first class to be allowed to give evidence in court, and permitted to settle on land secured to them and their children; but no one to be admitted to this class until he has been resident in Bencoolen three years. The second class to be employed in ordinary labour. The third class, or men of abandoned and profligate character, to be kept to the harder kinds of labour, and confined at night.

In cases of particular good conduct a prospect may be held out of emancipating deserving convicts from further obligation of services on condition of their supporting themselves and not quitting the settlement.

Upon the abstract question of the advantage of this arrangement I believe there will be little difference of opinion. The advantage of holding out an adequate motive of exertion is sufficiently obvious, and here it would have the double tendency of diminishing the bad characters and of increasing that of useful and industrious settlers, thereby facilitating the general police of the country and diminishing the expenses of the Company."

These intentions were acted upon afterwards, and the good effects of the regulations were soon apparent; a large body of people who had been living in the lowest state of degradation soon became useful labourers and happy members of society. So grateful were they for the change, that when they were sent round to Penang on the transfer of Bencoolen to the Dutch in 1825, as we have stated, they entreated to be placed on the same footing as they had been placed at Fort Marlborough, and not reduced to the state of the convicts in Prince of Wales Island, who were kept as a Government gang to be employed wherever their services might be thought most desirable.

Upon December 20th, 1823, Sir Stamford Raffles wrote a further letter to Government in regard to these convicts, of which we can only give an extract, which runs thus—

"As the management of convicts ought to be a subject of consideration, I send you a copy of the regulations established for those of this place. The convicts now at Bencoolen amount to 800 or 900, and the number is gradually increasing. They are natives of Bengal and Madras; that is to say, of those presidencies. The arrangement has been brought about gradually, but the system now appears complete, and, as far as we have yet gone, has been attended with the best effects. I have entrusted Mr. John Hull with the superintending of the department, and he feels great pleasure and satisfaction in the general improvement of this class of people."

It is greatly to be regretted that we have been unable to obtain a copy of the regulations to which Sir Stamford Raffles refers, but we have no doubt they formed the basis of what were hereafter called the "Penang rules."

It was, as we have said, in the year 1825 that the whole of the Bencoolen convicts were transferred to Penang, and thence, as opportunities offered later on, to Malacca and Singapore. One point we trace in regard to those convicts is that, greatly to their disappointment, they missed the freedom they had possessed at Bencoolen, for they were sent to work in gangs upon the roads, and in levelling ground near the town of Penang. At first they were tried at jungle cutting and burning, but had no aptitude for it. This work was therefore entrusted to Malays, who we all know have a natural bent for cutting down trees and underwood, and are possessed of implements wonderfully suited for the purpose.

We may remark here that transportation in those early times had its terrors both to the European from our shores to Australia, and to the native of India to these settlements, and more especially to the latter.

Though, by a system of "assignment" or "compulsory" servitude to masters, or by a ticket of leave which made it open to the European criminal to work for whom and where he pleased, expatriation became in time to be less severely felt; still, for a long period it continued to act as a deterrent to others, though to the convict himself it was "greater in idea perhaps than in reality." To the native of India it meant even a severer punishment than to the European, for to be sent across the "kala pani," or "black water," in a convict ship or "jeta junaza," or "living tomb" as they called it, meant, especially to a man of high caste, whether of the right or left hand section, the total loss to him of all that was worth living for. He could never be received in intercourse again with his own people, and so strong are the caste ideas of ceremonial uncleanness that it would be defilement to his friends and relations even to offer to him sustenance of any kind, and he was in point of fact excommunicated and avoided. Happily this dread of caste defilement has now, by railway communication over the country and equalization of classes under our rule, greatly diminished, but it is still, as Balfour says, "a prominent feature in every-day Hindu life." Sir Stamford Raffles' views as to the treatment of those transported convicts have in the main been recognised by all authorities in the Straits Settlements since his time; and his suggestion as to the privileges to be granted to men of the first class, though not defined by him as a "ticket of leave," has been all along kept in view, and was in regular force in the jail of which we treat. He divided his convicts into three classes only, but as time went on they were separated into six classes, and later on in the narrative will be given the reasons for this enlargement of the number. Dr. Mouat, Inspector General of Jails, Bengal, in a paper read before the Statistical Society some few years ago, spoke of this jail and the ticket-of-leave system as follows:—

"I visited the Straits Settlements in 1861 when under the rule of my friend, Sir Orfeur Cavenagh, and found in existence a system of industrial training of convicts superior to anything we had at that time on the continent of India. It was said to have been inaugurated by the celebrated Sir Stamford Raffles in 1825, when Singapore was first selected for the transportation of convicts from India, and to have been subsequently organised and successfully worked by General H. Man, Colonel MacPherson, and Major McNair. The ticket-of-leave system was in full and effective operation, and very important public works have been constructed by means of convict labour, chief amongst them St. Andrew's Cathedral, a palace for the Governor, and most of the roads. The ticket-of-leave convicts were said to be a well-conducted, industrious lot of men, who very rarely committed fresh crimes, who all earned an honest livelihood, and were regarded as respectable members of the community amongst whom they dwelt. The public works were creditable examples of prison industry and skill St. Andrew's Cathedral, built under Major McNair from plans prepared by Colonel MacPherson entirely by convict labour, struck me as one of the finest specimens of ecclesiastical architecture which I had seen in the East, and I believe there exists in no other country a more remarkable example of the successful industrial training of convicts."

We are not of course greatly concerned in this treatise with the original crimes committed by those Indian convicts, and for which they had received a sentence of transportation. Suffice it to say that their warrants showed generally that, in the case of convicts for life, the crimes were for the most part those of Murder, Thuggee, and Dacoity; while those sentenced to a term of years had been tried and convicted of frauds and forgeries, robbery with violence, and such like misdemeanours. "Thuggee," we all know, though it will bear repetition here, was in full operation all over India from very early times, but at the beginning of this century it engaged the serious attention of the Indian Government; and it was found to be an hereditary pursuit of certain families who worked in gangs—the Hindus to satisfy their goddess Bhawani, and other sects the goddess Devi—and they committed a countless number of murders all over the country. Thugs were a bold, resolute set of men, and as a rule divided themselves into groups consisting of a leader, a persuader, a strangler, a scout, and a gravedigger, but all the gangs, happily for India, were finally broken up under Colonel Sleeman about 1860. Some of the men were hanged, and many transported to our penal settlements in the Straits of Malacca. Dacoity was in some parts of India akin to Thuggee, for the leaders carried with them in the same way a sacred implement, which was devoted to Bhawani. In the case of the Thugs this was a pickaxe, but with the Dacoits it was an axe with a highly-tempered edge.

In the early days we talk of, it was the common practice of the authorities to brand these life convicts with a hot iron to indicate the character of their crime, and this was in some cases done upon the forehead both in the English language and in the vernacular of the district where the crime was committed. This was very properly put a stop to shortly after the custom became known. We have seen some of those in our jail who, by good conduct, have risen to a ticket of leave, using their utmost endeavours to get rid of the marks, but without effect; and finally as a last resource they were obliged to be content to hide the "stigma" by wearing their turbans, or head-dresses, inconveniently low down over their brows.

It is worthy of remark here, in reference to those native criminals who are in the habit of working in gangs, more especially among the Thugs, how signally they often fail when they attempt to act alone. Amongst our Thugs we had one (a strangler) who, coveting a pair of gold bangles on the wrist of a fellow-convict employed at the General Hospital, one night tried the handkerchief upon him, but missed his mark, and got away without being detected. Later on, the convict authorities examined the warrants of all the men at the hospital, and this gave them a clue, which they followed up successfully and caught the "Thug." He was punished, and then confessed, saying, "Bhawani was unkind, and I could not do it by myself; I missed my companions," or "saubutwalé" as he called them, literally meaning those "I kept company with."

It will not be inappropriate to mention here the callous and brutalized nature of those gang-robbers, of whom it is recorded that, when one of their gang was suddenly arrested, they at once decapitated him, and carried off the head, lest the whole gang should be betrayed.

Footnotes:

Literally, swollen at the source.

Chapter II

A SLIGHT SKETCH OF PENANG AND THE TREATMENT OF THE CONVICTS THERE

Penang, also named "Prince of Wales" Island as a compliment to the then Prince of Wales, afterwards George IV. This name for the island has become almost obsolete, and the Malay name Pi'nang, for the "Areka Palm," which flourishes there, is that by which it is now always known. It is situated at the northern extremity of the Malacca Straits, and was ceded to us by the Rajah of Kedah in 1785, when we gave up, but only for a time, our British settlement on the North Andaman, which we had acquired in 1789 and abandoned in 1796. Province Wellesley, opposite to Penang, upon the Malay Peninsula, was thirteen years later taken by us for the purpose of suppressing piracy, and forms part of this British settlement. The island has an area of 107 square miles, and the province of 270 square miles. Another dependency of the settlement since 1889 is the Dindings with the Island of Pangkor, where the treaty of 1874 was made by Sir Andrew Clarke, and which eventually led to our protectorate of several of the native states of the Malay Peninsula, and their complete federation in 1896.

FORT CORNWALLIS, PENANG.

Plate II.

When Penang was first occupied it was almost uninhabited, and the whole island was covered with the densest jungle, but it was not long before Captain Light, who was appointed the first Superintendent of Trade, made a road to the highest point of the island, then called "Bel retiro" but now Penang Hill. A great part of the island was soon cleared and roads made, so that in 1792, seven years after it came into our hands, Captain Light was able to report that the population had increased to 10,000 souls; this increase of population has been steadily going on from year to year, until, with its dependencies, Penang, after a little more than a century, now numbers no less than 240,000.

Since 1825, when the Indian convicts from Bencoolen were added to those already on the island, their labour was almost wholly turned to account in the construction of roads both on the island and in the province; but about 1850 some intramural work was also undertaken. The gangs in the province were at last taught to cut and burn the jungle as well as to construct the roads, and the records say at some risk from tigers which infested the province in those days, and occasionally carried off a straggler from the gangs at work. They were also bitten in large numbers by the venomous hamadryads which used to abound there, and from the poison of which some died.

About the time our treatise commences, Penang had acquired the monopoly of the trade of the Malayan Peninsula and Sumatra. It also had a large traffic with China, Siam, Borneo, the Celebes, and other places in the Eastern Archipelago; but after the establishment later on of Singapore it had begun to decline, and the settlement then became second only in commercial importance. But within the last quarter of a century the trade has considerably revived, owing largely to the planting of tobacco in Sumatra by European planters, and the annexation of the native states of the Malayan Peninsula, both of which have constituted Penang the chief shipping centre for their produce.

Before we pass on to treat of the Singapore jail, it will be well briefly to describe the method pursued in dealing with the Indian convicts on their first arrival in Penang, as far back as we can trace any definite notice in regard to them. They were confined at the outset in the then existing prison known as "Chowrusta Lines," situated on the Penang road; but this proving to be too small to accommodate all the convicts from India, a larger and more commodious prison was built on the opposite side of the road. It consisted of an enclosure, surrounded by a high brick wall, subdivided into yards, in each of which were erected the wards or dormitories. These were simply long rooms open to the high roof, having windows on either side secured by iron bars. Iron gates closed the doorways to each ward, which were locked at night. A gangway seven to eight feet wide ran the whole length of the ward, and sleeping platforms about seven feet wide extended to the full length of the ward on either side of this gangway. The hospital ward was similar to the others, except that it was a two-storied building, and cots were provided instead of the continuous sleeping platforms. The hospital and women's ward were all within the enclosure in a separate yard. Warders' and apothecary's quarters were provided at the main entrance to the prison. Cooking places for the different castes and latrines were constructed in each yard; a military guard room, food and clothing stores were also supplied. Little can be said in favour of this prison, as the wards were ill-ventilated, and the sanitary arrangements were very imperfect. All the prisoners were in a somewhat lax system of association, except those undergoing punishment in cells. Prior to the receipt of the convicts from Bencoolen, Penang itself, as a penal settlement, had already been supplied from India with a number of transported criminals of all tribes and castes, who were working in gangs under free warders; but from vacancies and dismissals, and the consequent inability to supply the place of these warders, where free labour of the kind required was not obtainable, an attempt was then made to enlist the services of well-behaved convicts to oversee their fellow-prisoners. But it does not appear to have at all succeeded at that time, and we have it on record that the Governor in Council at Penang, in the year 1827, deemed it necessary to revise the regulations under which these Indian convicts were controlled; and accordingly we learn that a committee was appointed to assemble at Penang in November, 1827, when a code of revised rules was drawn up, and the following comment was made by the committee as to the employment of convicts as warders: "With regard to the present system of employing convicts as tindals and sirdars, the committee think it very objectionable, as it is impossible that men so intimately connected with those over whom they are placed can exercise that authority and control which is so essential in the management of such a body of men as the convicts. The duties at present performed by these servants are provided for in the proposed increase to the establishment."

These rules, subsequently known as the "Penang Rules," received the sanction of the Governor in Council, and were sent for guidance to the Resident Councillor at Singapore, to which settlement some few convicts had already been sent. This remark of the Penang committee, which in all fairness we have quoted, was doubtless quite true at the time when it was penned, and when the system of employing prisoners as warders was in its infancy, and, moreover, when the whole prison discipline was acknowledged to be in more or less an indifferent state; but, as will hereafter be shown, it did not hold good when the system was well established, and the choice of warders was made from those classes best suited for the control of their fellow-prisoners, especially in the outstations, or "commands" as they were called, where gangs of convicts were placed under their control in the construction and repairs of roads or in stone-quarrying.

In these early days, no organised system of industrial employment appears to have been carried on in this Penang jail, and no intramural workshops of any kind were provided, the convicts being employed almost exclusively on extramural works, such as opening up roads on the Penang Hill and throughout the island, and in Province Wellesley; also in brick-making, felling timber, burning lime, and reclaiming mangrove swamps. The ground on which some portion of the present town is built was filled up by convict labour. Much later on, however, in the Fifties, rattan work was introduced into the prison, and easy chairs, lounging chairs, baskets, and other articles of a very substantial quality were manufactured and sold to the public at a higher price than that for which the same articles could be purchased in the town, but they were far superior both in the quality of rattan and in their make. About the year 1860, blacksmiths' and carpenters' shops were established in the prison, and on the different "commands" in the country districts.

The ordinary discipline of the jail was carried out in accordance with the "Penang Rules" referred to, and any breach of these rules was punished according to the nature of the offence, at the discretion of the Superintendent. There was then no formal investigation or inquiry into convict complaints or misdemeanours, and no records of them were kept with any show of regularity. It was only after the appointment of the late General Man as Resident Councillor of Penang, Captain Hilliard being Superintendent, that a manifest improvement in the management and control of the convicts took place, and especially in their industrial training. He brought with him the system in force in Singapore, and the new rules and regulations formed with the sanction of the Governor, then Colonel Butterworth, and which were an improvement on the old Penang rules, but were only at this time being tentatively carried out in Penang. By these rules the entire abolition of free warders was approved, and petty officers raised from amongst the convicts themselves fully established, though as the Governor himself said in his letter to the Resident Councillor of Singapore in August, 1854, "I had drawn up these rules as long ago as 1845 in the face of much opposition."

The late General Man held the appointment at Penang from 1860 until 1867, when the Straits Settlements were transferred to the Crown, and from Penang he went to the Andaman Islands to introduce there the system of convict management in force in the Straits Settlements; and with the view to uniformity of practice, the Government of India had previously deputed Major, now General, Forlong to prepare a code of rules based on those in force in the Singapore jail.

When the transfer was fully effected, the new office of Comptroller of Indian Convicts was created, and the whole of those Indian convicts in the three settlements were placed under his charge. The "Butterworth Rules" remained in force, with certain alterations and improvements, until the disestablishment of the whole department in 1873.

As many of the convicts were continued to be employed at Penang and Province Wellesley on roads and works at a distance from the main jail, it was necessary to provide accommodation for them in convict lines, or "commands," as we have said, pronounced "kumman" by the convicts. It will be interesting to give some particulars about them: They consisted of a stockaded fence, constructed of rough poles of wood from four to six inches in diameter, and from ten to twelve feet long, set perpendicularly in a trench about two feet deep, and placed close together, being secured longitudinally by adze-dressed poles nailed securely on the outside and along the top of them. The stockade enclosed an area sufficient for the erection of the dormitory, cooking place, and sheds for the bullocks employed in carts to convey road material, and for protection also against the possible attacks of wild animals. The walls of the dormitory were constructed in what is well known as "wattle and daub." They were made with stout stakes driven firmly into the ground at about one foot apart, twigs of trees were then interwoven, and the whole then thickly plastered with a mixture of clay and cowdung, and when this had become thoroughly dry it was coated with whitewash. This formed both a substantial, and at the same time a sanitary walling, which was frequently treated with a further coating of limewash made thin. The dormitories were ten feet high, with a continuous open grating of wooden bars at the top, under the eaves of the roof, for the purpose of complete ventilation. The sleeping platforms were raised three feet off the ground floor, which was covered with the same composition as that of the walls, and the building was roofed with thatch. In the centre of the dormitory an earthenware brazier of burning charcoal was always maintained day and night, and occasionally crude fragrant gum Benjamin was thrown upon it. The natives believe that an aromatic perfume exhaled by fire keeps off all noxious effluvia; and we certainly found that they were in better health from the use of this incense, and from the fresh plastering of the floor every morning with cowdung diluted with water, which is a common practice in most of the native huts in India. This was regularly kept up by two convicts of the invalid class, who also acted as caretakers. The entrance to the enclosure was secured by a stout gate, which, after the roll was called, was locked every night at nine o'clock. The number of convicts stationed on one "command" averaged about thirty, and they were under the charge of a responsible convict warder of the grade of a tindal, with a peon and two orderlies and a native "moonshi," or timekeeper, to keep account of work done, and to forward reports to the main jail. By a system of surprise visits both day and night occasionally, we rarely found that any irregularities occurred.

It has not been already mentioned that the local jails, or houses of correction, though according to law they were kept distinct from the convict jails at the several settlements, nevertheless were in their superintendence placed under the Superintendent of Convicts and convict petty officers. A good proportion of these local prisoners were employed upon extramural works, under the guard of these convict petty officers, who, being natives of India, had nothing in common with the Chinese and Malays who formed the bulk of these prisoners, and they kept them well under control, and allowed but few escapes, and, moreover, they were never found open to the taking of bribes from the prisoners' relations and friends, who now and again would attempt to offer them forbidden articles.

At Penang there were a considerable number of these Indian convicts upon ticket of leave, who gained their livelihood in a variety of ways. Some of them were the first to discover the palm known by the Malays as "Plas tikoos," and by botanists as the "Licuala acutifida," a small palm, ordinarily not higher than from five to six feet. From this palm, which grew mostly upon the Penang Hill, were constructed walking-sticks called "Penang lawyers," and the process of preparing them was very simple: the epidermis, or exterior coating, was scraped off with glass, and then the stick was straightened with fire, as is done by the Malays in preparing the Malacca canes. Several of these Penang lawyers were sold by the convicts on the spot, and many more were exported to Europe and America.

Footnotes:

There is an old legend in the island that Captain Light, in order to encourage the Malays in the work of cutting down the jungle, pointed a cannon in the direction in which he required it to be cleared, then he loaded it with powder, and instead of a shot he put in several dollars, and firing it off he called out to the Malays, "Now you may have all you can find."

It is said that the eager contest which ensued, of one endeavouring to get the money before another, led to a regular scramble, which considerably helped forward the work.

Now under the able management of Col. R. C. Temple, C.I.E.

Simpson, in his *Side Lights on Siberia*, uses "command" as denoting a jail outside of the prison walls.

View larger image

BOUNDARIES OF MALACCA, PORTUGUESE PERIOD
(From Godinho de Eredia's Work).

Plate III.

Chapter III

OLD MALACCA AND THE FIRST INTRODUCTION OF CONVICTS THERE

Authorities differ very considerably as to the origin of the name of this place. Some attribute it to the Malay name for a shrub which largely abounded near the shore, a sort of "Phyllanthus emblica" of the spurge order; others, again, ascribe it to a plant called the "Jumbosa Malaccensis," or "Malay apple tree" of the myrtle bloom order; others, again, say that the Javanese were the first to colonize the place about the year 1160 of our time, and that they gave it the name "Malaka," which in that language means "an exile," in memory of one "Paramisura" who came there as a fugitive from the kingdom of Palembang.

In the original manuscript of Godinho de Eredia, of date 1613, reproduced by Janssen in 1882, he says that "Paramisura," the first king of the Malays, settled on the coast near to the Bukit China River, which is close to the present town, and called it "Malaka," after the fruit of a tree which grew there. (See sketch from that old work, Plate IV.) Anyway, like all Malay history, it is full of obscurity, and it really does not concern us very much just now as to what it is really derived from, though it would be no doubt interesting to Malay scholars to pursue the inquiry.

We know, however, on the best authority, that it was the first settlement formed by a European power in those seas. The Portuguese, in their palmy days under Albuquerque, took it from a Malay Sultan, named Mahomed Shah, in 1511. They kept quiet possession of it for 134 years, when it fell into the hands of the Dutch, who held it for seventy-four years; then the British took possession in 1795, restored it to the Dutch in 1818, who gave it back in 1824, and we have held it ever since. In size it is forty-two miles long and from eight to twenty-five miles broad, and contains 659 square miles.

In the old Portuguese days it was a very important place of trade, so much so that De Barros, their famous historian, wrote of it that, "the native town was a good league in length along the shore, and that there were many merchant vessels there from Calicut, Aden, Mecca, Java, and Pegu, and other places." This splendid trade, however, began to decline in the time of the Dutch, and shortly after we had opened Penang in 1785 it had almost entirely vanished.

View larger image

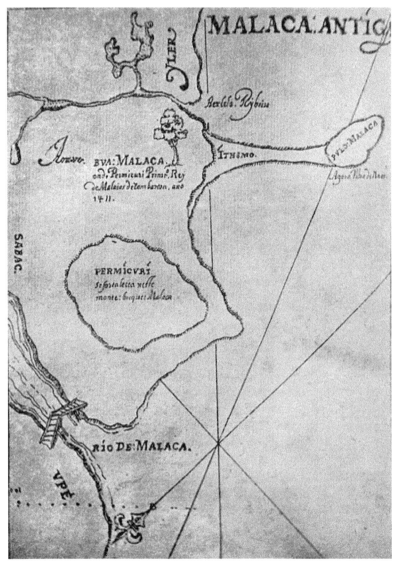

OLD MALACCA
(From Godinho de Eredia's Work).

Plate IV.

ALBUQUERQUE
(From Godinho de Eredia's Work).

Plate V.

The Portuguese must have attached great value to this their first settlement in what was then known as the "Golden Chersonese," for they spent vast sums of money in fortifying it, and enclosed a considerable enceinte by a wall of great height and thickness, and crowned the small hill of St. Paul's within by the erection of a fine cathedral dedicated to our Lady Del-Monte, with a monastery annexed to it. These fortifications were afterwards razed to the ground, and some of the old foundations may still be seen; but we left the buildings standing and the greater part of the cathedral to go to ruins. Some of the tombstones in the old nave bear the date 1515, and there is a tomb to the two Bishops of Japan, but there is nothing to indicate that the saintly St. Francis Xavier laboured here beyond a small tablet; but the memory of his deeds is yet fresh amongst the traditions of the Portuguese descendants still resident there.

Seen from the sea in these days, Malacca looks an antiquated old place, with all the signs of desertion about it. The old ruins on the hill form the most prominent feature in the landscape, and the once busy river (see Plate VI.)

is now almost closed even to boat traffic by the silt which has been brought down from the interior. It is difficult indeed to realize that this strange, dim old place was once the centre of a thriving trade from so many distant countries, though it still carries on its cultivation of rice and other grain, and this is yearly being more developed.

As far as we can gather, the first batch of convicts were sent to this place from Penang shortly after we took possession, and that they were employed in filling up the moat to suit it and the glacis for a parade ground. These convicts were confined first of all in the town jail, which was situated on the steep or eastern side of St. Paul's Hill, and was in point of fact the old Portuguese soldiers' barrack, and was constructed on a terrace excavated from the hillside; and, together with a hospital, warders' quarters, store rooms and other necessary buildings, was surrounded by a high wall built from the stone from the old fort ramparts. The few local prisoners were put into the old Dutch prison, and both these prisoners and the convicts were placed under the charge of half-blood Portuguese warders. For some years few convicts were sent into the interior, their labour being required for the public works in and near the town; but about the year 1840, as fresh arrivals came from Penang, which is about 250 miles north of it, gangs were made up to keep in repair about 100 miles of the public roads that were left to us, and to open up new communications near the frontier; so that we now have nearly 300 miles to keep in order. They were located in temporary huts surrounded by a palisading, and warders were raised from amongst the best behaved to be responsible for their work and general supervision. This practice was continued with satisfactory results, and gradually was introduced into the town jail, and the half-bred Portuguese warders were dismissed.

MALACCA RIVER IN 1870.

Plate VI.

ST. FRANCIS XAVIER
(From Godinho de Eredia's Work).

Plate VII.

Prior to the appointment to Malacca of Captain Man as Resident Councillor, but little had been done in the way of training the convicts in industrial occupation, but he established a few workshops and started them in various trades. It was not, however, until 1860 that anything approaching to really skilled labour could be got out of them. They were then supplied with good tools and an instructor, also a convict, was sent down from Singapore. After this, carts for the roads, iron and wood work for bridges, roofing timbers for public works, and other necessary requirements for the erection of minor works were satisfactorily accomplished. For some classes of work the convicts were superior to the Chinese workmen in the town, especially in metal turning and fitting. One Cingalese convict became so expert at this trade that upon his release from confinement he established himself in Ceylon, and has been doing a very profitable business, and occupies now a respectable position in life.

As far as can be gathered from the records, the convicts were, as a rule, well behaved, though in the early Sixties, owing to their maltreatment by an overseer who had the supervision of a gang for clearing the jungle and making roads upon Cape Rachado for the erection of a lighthouse, an *emeute* took place, and some life was lost, and many escaped inland, but were subsequently returned by the native Malay chiefs.

Some of the Indian convicts here on ticket of leave were expert shikarries, and frequently with their trained dogs would hunt the deer and wild boar, and dispose of the flesh to Chinese in the town at some profit to themselves.

In 1873, when the convict establishments in the Straits Settlements were finally broken up, those convicts still wanting time to complete their sentences were transferred to Singapore for transmission to the Andamans, those upon ticket of leave being permitted to merge into the population.

View larger image

TOWN AND ENVIRONS OF SINGAPORE IN 1878.

Plate VIII.

Chapter IV

A RUNNING HISTORY OF SINGAPORE: ITS JAIL SYSTEM AND ADMINISTRATION

The origin of the name of this island it is difficult to trace, but the generally accepted derivation is from the Sanscrit words, "Singh," a lion, and "Pura," a city or town; and if so, it would not have been given by the Malays, but more probably by the Indians, who, according to native history, came over with one, Rajah Suran, and conquered Johore and this island in about the year A.D. 1160. "Singh" is a title adopted by the Hindus, and by several military castes of Northern India, and the word "Singhpur" is often used by them to mean the grand entrance gate to a palace.

If, on the other hand, we assume that the Malays conferred the name to the island, they would in all probability have given it from their word "Singgah," which means "a place to stop at," or "to bait by the way," and as the embouchure of the Singapore river formed a commodious and sheltered retreat for their rowing and sailing prahus, this view is not inappropriate, the more especially as the affix "pura," meaning a city, had been known to them from the earliest times, and of which we have one instance at least from their original home of Sumatra, in the naming of their kingdom of Indrapura, which was, as Marsden says, "for a long time, from 1400 A.D., the seat of a monarchy of some consideration and extent."

The island is about twenty-seven miles long by fourteen broad, and contains an area of 206 square miles, and therefore is somewhat larger than the Isle of Wight. It is separated from the mainland of Johore by what is known as "The Old Straits," from its having been the only channel used in the early days by vessels bound eastward. The island was first settled upon, according to Balfour, "in A.D. 1160, by one Sri Sura Bawana," and from an inscription on a sandstone rock at the mouth of the Singapore River, now unfortunately destroyed, it would appear that Rajah Suran, of Amdan Nagara, after conquering the state of Johore with certain natives of India (Klings), proceeded in 1201 to a country then called "Tamask," and afterwards returned to "Kling," leaving the stone inscription in memory of his visit and victory. To have conquered Johore, the Rajah's vessels must have sailed by the Old Straits; but we have no record as to where "Tamask" was situated, and it is not given in the oldest Atlases we have been able to consult, viz. by D'Anville and others, though it may be in the charts of the 14th and 15th centuries. It seems more probable that the expedition set out from Java or Sumatra, to which places Hindus had, as we know, in very remote times proceeded from India, as the old ruins they have left there of their temples, supposed to be of the 7th century, plainly prove.

Sir Stamford Raffles, as we have already stated when treating of Bencoolen, took up the appointment of Lieutenant-Governor of that settlement on the 22nd March, 1818, and he had not been there long before he recognized the fact that British interests needed a trading centre somewhere in the Straits of Malacca. It was, he said, "not that any extension of territory was necessary, but the aim of Government should be to acquire somewhere in the Straits a commercial station with a military guard, and that, when once formed, it was his belief that it would soon maintain a successful rivalry with a neighbouring Power, who would be obliged either to adopt a liberal system of free trade, or see the trade of these seas collected under the British flag."

It is well known how the port of Rhio, on the west coast of the island of Bintang, which is separated from the island of Battam by the Rhio Strait, was first thought of; but we were too late in occupying it. Then the Carrimon Islands were suggested by the Resident Councillor of Malacca, at that time Major Farquhar; but the harbour was too exposed to the prevailing monsoon. Subsequently Tanjong Jatti, on the island of Bengkalis, was deemed to be a suitable site, but this had its objection as to situation; and after coasting about these seas for some little time, Sir Stamford Raffles finally fixed upon the island of Singapore for an entrepot for trade, and the wisdom and sagacity displayed by him in this selection has been abundantly proved.

Sir Stamford Raffles concluded the treaty with the native chiefs for the cession of the island to Great Britain, and the British flag was planted on the island on the same day that the treaty was signed, viz., the 19th February, 1819, but it has since been found to have been actually signed on the 6th of that month.

Our new possession, some 600 miles from Batavia, then contained in round numbers about 120 Malays and 30 Chinese. Some of these lived wholly in their boats at the mouth of the river, and the remainder in huts at Teloh Blangah, on the south side of the island. In the course of a year the population had risen to 5,000, and in little more than five years to 19,000 or 20,000 of all nations actively engaged in commerce, "offering to each and all a handsome livelihood and abundant profit." When the census was taken in 1881 the population had risen to 139,208, and in 1891 there was an increase of 45,346, making a total of 184,554, representing nearly every nationality and tribe in the Indian Archipelago, China, and India, and about 1,500 Europeans.

In the year 1822, the first settlers to dwell on the island were traders in the Archipelago, and they lived in raft houses, so called, or more probably in huts, erected on poles in the Malay style, and these were located on the site of the present "Commercial Square," which was then little more than a mud flat covered by the sea at high water. One of the first steps taken by the Government was to fill up this low-lying sea marsh, which was executed by free labour, but was subsequently largely assisted by some local prisoners who were confined in a temporary jail near by, on the site where the present Court-house now stands. The first magistrates to be appointed in the settlement, and who tried and sentenced these prisoners, were men whose names will ever be preserved unforgotten by the colony, and we make no excuse in giving them in full as obtained from *The Anecdotal History*, viz., Messrs. A. L. Johnstone, D. A. Maxwell, D. F. Napier, A. F. Morgan, John Purvis, Alexander Guthrie, E. Mackenzie, W. Montgomery, Charles Scott, John Morgan, C. R. Read, and Andrew Hay. Two magistrates sat in court with the Resident Councillor, to decide cases both civil and criminal, and juries were formed of five Europeans, or four Europeans and three leading natives. This court sat once a week, but a court of two magistrates sat twice a week to try cases, their office being open daily to hear complaints.

The insecurity of the temporary prison mentioned above, and the defects in its control, led to changes in its structure and general management. The Resident, then Mr. J. Crawford, expended $900 towards the construction of a more substantial building for the local prisoners, the transmarine convicts from Bencoolen and India having not yet arrived in the settlement. In April, 1823, as there was a great difficulty in obtaining free labour, the local prisoners were ordered to work upon the public roads.

When finally leaving the settlement, Sir Stamford Raffles entered into a new agreement with the Sultan and Tummongong of Johore, by which the whole of the island of Singapore and the adjacent islands were to be considered as entirely British territory. He considered this fresh agreement necessary on account of some peculiar ideas that were held at the time by certain dissentients.

On his final departure from Singapore, Sir Stamford Raffles received an address from the European and native merchants of Singapore, from which we quote the following significant extract:

"To your unwearied zeal, your vigilance, and your comprehensive views, we owe at once the foundation and maintenance of a settlement, unparalleled for the liberality of the principles on which it has been established— principles, the operation of which has converted in a period short beyond all example a haunt of pirates into the abode of enterprise, security, and opulence."

Sir Stamford replied with his characteristic modesty in a letter dated Singapore, June 9th, 1823. The letter is too long to quote *in extenso*, but we give the following extracts from it. After acknowledging the receipt of their address, and remarking upon the impossibility of his being indifferent to any of the interests, especially the commercial interests, of Singapore, under the peculiar circumstances of his connection with the establishment of the settlement, he says, "It has happily been consistent with the policy of Great Britain, and accordant with the principles of the East India Company, that Singapore should be established as a 'free port,' and that Singapore will long, and always remain a free port, and that no taxes on trade or industry will be established to check its future rise and prosperity, I can have no doubt." "I am justified in saying thus much on the authority of the Supreme Government of India, and on the authority of those who are most likely to have weight in the councils of our nation at home."

Referring to difficulties which had to be encountered on the establishment of the freedom of the port, he says, "In the commanding station in which my public duty has placed me, I have had an opportunity of, in a great measure, investigating and determining the merits of the case, and the result renders it a duty on my part, and which I perform with much satisfaction, to express my most unqualified approbation of the honourable principles which actuated the merchants of Singapore on that occasion."

We give the above extracts to show the rapid advance that had been made in the first five years of the settlement's existence, owing mainly to the sagacity, forethought, and wisdom of its eminent founder, and we have added the population up to this period to show its steady rise and progress.

It was, however, in January, 1824, that the first regular census was taken. The population then consisted of 74 Europeans, 16 Armenians, 15 Arabs, 4,580 Malays, 3,317 Chinese, 756 natives of India, and 1,925 Bugis, making a total of 10,683. It was in this year that Singapore was first mentioned in the House of Commons, in a remark made by Mr. Canning, who had been nominated Governor-General of India in 1822, but did not go out to that country, that "Singapore in six years would produce spices sufficient for the consumption of Great Britain and her colonies"—a prophecy not yet fulfilled.

In May of the same year the Resident made a voyage round the island in the ship *Malabar*, 380 tons burden, to view the boundary of the island and to take formal possession; and it was while on this voyage that the British flag was planted on the island of "Pulo Obin," an island which has since largely supplied the town of Singapore with granite for making roads and also for building purposes. The Government quarries situated upon it were subsequently worked almost entirely by transmarine convicts, of which more will be said hereafter.

ORIGINAL HUTS FOR CONVICTS, SINGAPORE
(From *Life of Sir Stamford Raffles*).

Plate IX.

On the 18th of April, 1825, the first batch of convicts transported from India to Bencoolen were transferred from there to Singapore. They arrived in the brig *Horatio*, and consisted of 80 convicts transported from Madras, of whom 73 males and 1 female were for life, and 6 male convicts on short sentences. On the 25th of the same month another batch was received, also convicts from Bencoolen. These consisted of 122 convicts transported from Bengal, of whom 88 males and 1 female were for life, and 33 for short terms. When these Indian convicts were landed at Singapore they were placed at first in an open shed, or godown (from the Malay word "godong," a shed), which stood on the site where the present public offices stand, with only four free petty officers, or "peons," natives of Chittagong in the Bengal presidency, in charge of them. Subsequently temporary buildings, to contain 1,200 to 2,000 convicts, were erected near the Hindu temple, then situated near the Brass Basa Canal, and at a considerable cost it is given as £13,199 (see Plate IX.). They were all located in these sheds, and there was little or no prison control over them; only, occasionally, an officer of the police came and called the roll in order to report to Government that all were present. These convicts were afterwards detailed to the work of filling up the mud flat before referred to as the site of the present "Commercial Square." For this purpose they carried the soil from near the Hindu temple and from Pearls Hill. Mr. Bonham, the Resident, finding that the convicts worked willingly, and were well behaved, discharged the free "peons," or warders, and selected five Madrasees and five Bengalees from their number to supervise their fellow-convicts. This was, as far as we gather, the first trial of the system of convict warders at Singapore, possibly the first venture of the kind made in any penal establishment. As convicts continued to arrive from India, many of those from Bencoolen were constituted warders over their fellows, in the proportion of one warder to every twenty convicts. Each warder was granted a monthly wage of $3.00 in addition to his rations and clothing, with the usual blanket given to each convict once a year. In addition to his ordinary rations, clothing, and annual blanket, each convict received a monthly allowance of 50 cents (say 2s.) a month, to purchase condiments and salt. A European overseer was placed in immediate charge of the convicts, and a Superintendent over the whole convict establishment, this responsible duty first falling upon Lieutenant Chester, of the Bengal Native Infantry.

The convicts from Bencoolen were not sent over to the Straits of Malacca in chains, but those received from India in the earliest times were manacled with light leg fetters, in which they had to work for a probationary period of three months. As, however, they were granted, equally with the others, the privilege of going about the town to make their purchases, it is said they ceased to consider their fetters a mark of degradation, being so completely overwhelmed with the thought of banishment from their country and kindred; and to many men of caste it must be remembered that transportation alone was a severe punishment.

In the year 1826 there was a change of government in the settlements. Hitherto the settlements of Penang, Malacca, and Singapore had not been incorporated under one government. In this year it was decided by the Supreme Government to do so, and the seat of government was fixed at Penang, that being our oldest settlement in these seas. On this change taking place, many more of the Indian convicts from Penang were sent down to Singapore, the ship *Esperanza* bringing down a further batch of 23 Bengal life convicts (males), and 26 Madras convicts (males), and 1 female; 31 Bombay (males), and 2 female convicts.

From the accounts given in the newspapers of that day, the convicts were at this time treated with great indulgence if of proved good behaviour, being permitted, after their work was over, to engage themselves as servants to the residents, who, in the scarcity of labour at that time, and the fitness of the convicts for such service, were content to give them a very liberal wage. In the early days of penal colonies this has not infrequently occurred, and some of these old convicts have been known to amass considerable sums of money, and, indeed, to become possessed of landed property in the town. The Government, however, under Major Campbell, who succeeded Lieutenant Chester, took care to exact from them a large amount of useful work in the filling up of swampy ground near the town, and laying out plots of land for building purposes. They also blasted the rocks at the mouth of the Singapore river, on the site of which was afterwards constructed a fort, named after the first Resident, Mr. Fullerton, and much of the rock was also used in the construction of the sea and river walls adjoining. Their services were also turned to account on any occasion when the presence of a body of men under discipline was required, such as the suppression of fires. An instance is given in the journal already quoted of a serious outbreak of fire in Market Street, in the year 1830, which threatened to consume the houses in several streets adjoining. There were no fire engines in those days, and the only supply of water was carried in buckets by the convicts, which materially helped to subdue it. The houses in the square at the back of Market Street were not burnt; they, and also the houses on the side of Market Street next the square, were partly built of brick, but those on the opposite side were wholly of wood, and were quickly destroyed. The middle of the square was covered with goods carried from the burning houses.

Occasionally, even in those days, convicts were employed as orderlies and servants to public officers, and when Dr. Oxley's house was attacked by burglars in 1821, his Indian convict servant, though wounded by a "kris," succeeded in capturing the burglar, who turned out to be a Malay pirate from Bencoolen. Robbery on land was not common amongst Malays in those days, but piracy was one of their pastimes, and their romances always glorify their ancestors in this pursuit.

The rules at that time in force amongst the convicts were what were known as the "Penang Rules," already mentioned, and published in 1827; but there were also a few scattered rules known as the "Bencoolen Rules," probably some of those drawn up by Sir Stamford Raffles, and referred to in his letter of the 20th September, 1823, and incorporated with the former.

In 1832 an alteration in the seat of government took place. Penang had hitherto been the seat of government, but in this year it was transferred to Singapore, which had by this time become the most important of the three Settlements.

When later on, in the year 1833, Mr. G. D. Coleman was placed in charge of the convicts as "Surveyor and Executive Officer of Government," a great improvement was set on foot in the regular and systematic employment of these convicts. He, by their means, reclaimed large plots of land as intakes from the sea and river marshes, and largely extended the town lots, so that Captain Begbie, who in that year wrote a book upon the Straits Settlements, stated that "200 of these convicts, in eight months, at a small money outlay of $500 for covered drains, had reclaimed 28 acres of marsh, and intersected it with roads. This land was shortly afterwards sold at a handsome price, and was very quickly covered with good, substantial upper-story houses, which were readily let."

Under Mr. Coleman the public roads on the sea front were marked out and constructed, and also the main road from the town to Campong Glam, now known as North and South Bridge Roads. He surveyed and marked out the first country road towards Bukit Timah, and he afterwards laid out the Serangoon, the New Harbour, Budoo, and Thompson's Roads, and employed Indian convicts principally in their construction. When the convicts could not be marched out to and from their daily work to the prison, owing to the long distance they had to traverse, Mr. Coleman constructed for them temporary buildings, surrounded by a fence, similar to those already described when treating of Province Wellesley and Malacca. In these "commands" they were located until the work on which they were employed was completed; and in many cases these "commands," as they were always called, became permanent stations for the convicts employed in maintaining the roads. At first their rations were sent out to them from town once a month, but subsequently it was found desirable for them to attend the general muster at the main prison on the first of every month, and to receive their rations then, and to be inspected at the same time by the Superintendent.

The records of the jail at this time, and until the year 1844, have not been kept, as we have said, with any precision, and, indeed, most of them are missing; but the excellent work performed by Mr. Coleman (in the execution of which he, as far as possible, employed convict labour) is, fortunately, to be seen in the map of the town and its environs surveyed by him in 1836, and lithographed in Calcutta the same year, a copy of which is given in Moor's Notices of the Indian Archipelago.

Mr. Coleman was no mean architect. It was he who designed the first church for Singapore. It was erected on the site where the present cathedral stands. It was completed in 1837, and consecrated in September, 1838, but was opened for service on the 18th June, 1837, by the first chaplain appointed from Bengal, the Rev. Edmund White. Indian convicts were employed in the erection of this church, chiefly as labourers, as they were also at the public buildings which were erected about this time, notably the first extension of the Raffles Institution and its museum.

To Mr. Coleman, however, the colony is chiefly indebted for the many excellent roads on the island, and the carrying out of the disposition of town allotments, projected in the first instance by Sir Stamford Raffles himself, in his instructions to the Committee appointed for the purpose shortly after the settlement was founded.

Mr. G. D. Coleman died on the 27th March, 1885, and the newspapers of the day, in regretting his death, brought about by hard work and exposure in the public service, spoke in the highest terms of his ability as an architect and surveyor, and Superintendent of Convicts.

Chapter V

SINGAPORE (*Continued*)

There were then about 1,100 or 1,200 Indian convicts in Singapore, divided into six classes, and employed in various ways as already narrated, but the following extract from *The Anecdotal History* is worth quoting verbatim:

"Singapore, Malacca, Penang, and Maulmein were the Sydneys of India. There are upon an average about 1,100 to 1,200 native convicts from India constantly at Singapore. These are employed making roads and digging canals; and, undoubtedly, without them the town, as far as locomotion is concerned, would have been now but a sorry residence. They are secured within high walls, and although a few now and then escape, they meet with such rough treatment from the Malays on the Peninsula, that they find it commonly the most prudent course to return, or allow themselves to be brought back. The native of India accommodates himself more easily to banishment than a European does, because his ideas lead to predestination, and his habits are simple. In former days, when convict discipline was not so well understood as it is now, the convicts transported from India used to traffic and amass money; banishment was in some cases, perhaps, sought for, and crimes were, it is feared, sometimes committed by natives to obtain it; but the felon must now expect to be kept in his place and hard at work. Still, the convict whose period is short, contrives to save something out of his allowance, and on the expiration of his term he generally sets up as a keeper of cattle, or a letter-out of carriages and horses; and undoubtedly some of these men are as well, if not better behaved than many of their native neighbours of higher pretensions. There are regulations by which the convict is encouraged by certain rewards, or remission short of emancipation, to orderly conduct."

When Mr. Coleman resigned, the duties of Superintendent were taken up by Captain Stevenson of the 12th Madras Native Infantry, who carried out the system then in force, and somewhat added to the strength of the convict warders; for we find in his annual report for 1845 the following remarks: "Convict peons are selected from the second class for general good conduct and intelligence, and they continue to receive $3 each per mensem, in addition to provisions and clothing. Free peons were, I hear, formerly tried, but found not to be so well suited for the peculiar duties required of them; besides, the prospect of gaining a belt—a mark of authority—is a strong inducement to good conduct on the part of the convict, and conduces much towards lightening, in the well disposed, the feeling of hopelessness that ever accompanies a sense of imprisonment and slavery for life."

At this time (1840 to 1845), Singapore was more than ever before infested with tigers—it is supposed that they swam across the narrow part of the Old Straits, from Johore to Kranji. The number of natives, principally Chinese, employed on gambier and pepper farms, that were carried off or destroyed by them annually was considerable, and it was said at the time that not a day passed without one man being killed by wild animals. Whether it was actually so or not, there are no police statistics to prove, but as many as five in eight days were reported at that time, and in later years, about 1860, as many as 200 deaths were notified to the police in one year, and probably a great number never were brought to notice, because the difficulty of obtaining coolies to work in the thick jungle, as it then was, was a great inducement to the "Towkays," or Head Chinese, to keep the number of deaths as much as possible from being known. In those days a reward of one hundred dollars was offered by Government for every tiger brought to the police station, whether alive or dead; and this sum, owing to their continued ravages, was subsequently increased to one hundred and fifty dollars.

One seizure of a man-eater is worth recording here; it is taken from *The Singapore Free Press* of the year 1840, and runs as follows:—

"The news of the capture and death of a tiger last Saturday night on a Chinaman's plantation, close to that of Mr. Balustier, the American Consul, gave general satisfaction, being the first of these destructive animals which the Chinese had succeeded in catching alive. A pit was dug where his track had been observed, the mouth of which was covered lightly over, and two or three dogs tied as bait. The ruse luckily took effect, and, when advancing to his imagined prey, he was himself precipitated into the pit head foremost, where he was very soon despatched by the natives, who pounded him to death with stones. He was a large animal for the Malay type, measuring 9 ft. 3 in. from the nose to the tip of the tail, which was 35 inches long, the circumference round the forearm being 21 inches. The captors have claimed and obtained from the local authorities the promised reward of one hundred dollars, besides having sold the flesh of the animal itself to the Chinese, Klings, and others for six fanams a catty (a fanam is about three halfpence), by which they realized about seventy dollars more."

It is singular how all natives believe that by eating the flesh of the tiger they absorb the essence or distinctive features of the animal. Balfour says that "the clavicle or collar-bone of the tiger is considered of great virtue by many natives of India. The whiskers are supposed by some to endow their possessor with unlimited power over the opposite sex." Tiger bones are often sold in China to form an ingredient in certain invigorating jellies, made of hartshorn, and the plastron of the terrapin or tortoise. Burmese and Malays eat the flesh of the tiger, because they believe that by eating it they acquire the courage and sagacity of the animal. Tigers' claws are used as charms, and the most solemn oath of one of the aboriginal tribes of India, the "Santals," is sworn when touching a tiger's skin; handsome brooches and earrings are also made from tigers' claws mounted in gold. In 1854 no less than six persons were killed within the space of a few days not far from the town, and in April of that year the Government, alarmed for the safety of the people, sanctioned a considerable expenditure for the construction of tiger pits over many parts of the island. In August of the same year the following article appeared in *The Singapore Free Press:*—

"The attention of His Honour the Governor having been directed to the continued deplorable ravages committed by tigers on the island, he has expressed himself ready to adopt any measures which may tend to remove the evil. It has been suggested that persons are to be found in the vicinity of Calcutta trained for the purpose of destroying tigers; and His Honour has written to the Bengal Government requesting that half a dozen of these 'shikarries' should be sent to the Straits for a limited period, to be employed in the destruction of these animals. The Governor has also directed that in the meantime, should it be deemed expedient, a certain number of volunteers from convicts of the third class should be permitted to beat the jungle once every month with tom-toms (native drums), horns, etc., which, if they do not lead to the destruction of the tigers, may frighten them away from the island, to which they come from the neighbouring state of Johore."

Later, in 1859, finding that the number of tigers on the island, and the number of people killed by them, were still increasing, the Governor, General Sir Orfeur Cavenagh, discussed the matter with the then Superintendent of Convicts (Major McNair), who informed him that he had good shikarries amongst the Indian convicts, and it was arranged to organize parties of convicts for their destruction. Three parties, of three men in each party, were selected, and armed with the old muzzle-loading muskets and ball ammunition. One party was sent to the Bukit Timah or Central district, another to the Serangoon and Changi or Eastern district, and the third to the Choo Choo Kang or Western district. These parties were generally successful in killing half a dozen or so in the course of the year, chiefly in the Central or garden district. Recourse was also had to trapping them in cleverly-constructed deep pits, built cone-wise, and by heavy beams of timber suspended from tree to tree over their tracks, connected on the ground with springes; but only upon rare occasions were they successful in this way. We had in our possession several skins and skulls from those destroyed by convicts. Some castes amongst these convicts from India, when employed on this duty, were also very expert in catching such venomous snakes as cobras and craits. They appeared not to possess the slightest dread of them, and would stealthily follow them to their burrows, then grasp the tail, and by a rapid movement of the other hand along the body to just below the head, grip the snake firmly at the neck and allow it to coil round their arm. During the construction of Fort Canning, later on, many were so caught and brought down to the jail for the reward. They were then destroyed, the convicts at the time always asking pardon of the snake for so betraying it to their masters. It is worth mentioning here that in the jail there were so many different races of India, and men of so many occupations and artifices, that what a man of one caste did not know, another would be sure to volunteer to perform. This collection of such a variety of races in a jail under the association system had another and more important advantage, for it was at once a safeguard and protection against any possible combined revolt against the authorities, for one caste would invariably "split" against another.

It was in the year 1841 that it was decided to erect a jail for the Indian convicts on a site near the Brass Basa Canal on the east of the town, and immediately below Government Hill, now known as Fort Canning. The boundary wall was first built, and then a brick building within, which was subsequently used as a convict hospital. This is shown in the plan of the whole prison made in 1872, a copy of which is given later. In this brick building the defaulters and those in irons were placed on one side, and the local prisoners on the other. The remainder of the convicts were lodged in temporary structures inside the enclosure wall; and those employed in positions of trust were allowed to erect small huts for themselves in the style of a native village just outside the wall, in which they were allowed to have their wives and families. There was but one entrance to this enclosure, where convict warders were at all times stationed as a gate guard. It will be readily understood that discipline could not well be maintained under such circumstances, while no records appear to have been kept of any kind, relating to their daily employment or occupation, so there is nothing to show whether the convicts were employed in the erection of this boundary wall; but it is more probable that they were only used as labourers, and not as artisans, for it was not until a later date that they were organized and trained as skilled workmen.

It may be well for us to indicate here the progress made in the Singapore town up to 1842, as given by *The Free Press* newspaper in that year. It runs thus:—

"A stranger visiting Singapore cannot fail to be struck by the signs everywhere exhibited of the settlement being in a high state of prosperity and progressive improvement. If he lands on the side next the town he beholds the pathway in front of the merchants' 'godowns' or warehouses cumbered with packages, and if he glances inside one of the 'godowns' he will see it filled with packages and bales of goods from all parts of the world. If he goes among the native shops he finds them filled with clamorous Klings (natives of the Coromandel Coast of India) and Chinese, all busily engaged in driving bargains. Passing on, he comes to where, near the jail, the swamp is being filled up and covered with shops, which are seen in every stage of progress, some with the foundations newly laid, and others nearly completed. If he wishes to leave the town he crosses the Singapore River by a new bridge, which was built two years ago. The scene now undergoes a change: in place of the narrow and crooked streets the stranger finds himself amongst rows of neat villas, each standing in its own enclosure. The Governor's residence is to the left upon a small hill commanding a fine view of the town and harbour. The flag-staff is also placed there, and at all hours of the day may be seen covered with flags, announcing the approach of ships from every quarter of the globe. If he should go into the country, the many thriving plantations of spices and other tropical productions (amongst which are to be noted one or two sugar estates) present an equally pleasing sight, and give promise of a long continuance to the well-being of the settlement."

In this year, 1842, or it may perhaps have been in the previous year, Mr. J. T. Thompson came to Singapore in the capacity of Government Surveyor; whereupon the Government called upon all holders and occupiers of land to point out to him their boundaries, preparatory to the issue of proper leases. Under his direction there was a systematic survey made of all allotments upon the island; and intelligent Indian convicts were provided him to act as his survey party, being preferred for that duty over freemen to be obtained in the town. These convicts formed the nucleus of a regular native staff for this department of the Government; and, indeed, up to the time of the abolition of the jail they continued to be employed as chainmen and survey assistants.

When Mr. Thompson visited Malacca, to inquire into the system pursued there, he found it to be of the most primitive type. For the linear measurements the surveyor had for a chain, rattans jointed together, and this, with a ten-foot rod and a common compass, formed their whole equipment. When he tested however the measurements of the fields and the town lots, he was surprised to find to what approach to accuracy they had arrived with their rude implements. Indian convicts were also there employed as land measurers and assistants.

Upon his return to Singapore, Mr. Thompson designed a European hospital, and adjoining it a pauper hospital, erected mostly at the cost of a benevolent Chinese gentleman of the name of Tan-Tock-Seng. They were built on a plateau of Pearls Hill facing the town. Some years later these buildings were required for military purposes, and were adapted for the purposes of a Commissariat and Ordnance Department respectively. A new building, in which was incorporated a general hospital, was subsequently erected facing the Bukit Timah Road, and the Tan-Tock-Seng hospital for paupers was built further outside the town on the Serangoon Road. In the erection of these buildings convict labour was very largely utilised, and in the front elevation of Tan-Tock-Seng's hospital they had some rather difficult mouldings to execute.

In the year 1844, owing to the amount of building that was then going on in the town, there was a great dearth of bricks; so much so, that the Chinese brick-kilns could not supply the immense demand, and the price per laksa of 10,000 rose more than fifty per cent. This led to the determination on the part of the Government to make their own bricks, and an order was issued to the Public Works Department to arrange for their manufacture by the convicts. This was subsequently done; and a suitable site having been found upon the Serangoon Road, a large establishment was started, an account of which will be given in detail when we come to deal with the industrial occupations of the Indian convicts. The first Government brick-field, however, was started at Rochore, under Captain Faber, but was given up after only a short trial. He employed free labour.

Chapter VI

SINGAPORE (*Continued*)

During the year 1845 the Bukit Timah Road was opened up by convict labour between Bukit Timah and Kranji, so that the produce hitherto carried by water to Singapore from the neighbouring country of Johore could now be brought into town by road, while at the same time land was thus opened up for cultivation. The convicts were also employed in this year in constructing a road to the summit of Telok Blangah Hill, now called Mount Faber, for the purpose of building there a signal station, that upon the island of Blakan Mati having proved unhealthy, due, as it was said at the time, to malaria from the enclosed marsh at the back of the island, and to the tainted air from decaying pine-apple leaves, which were left by the Malays, who cultivated the fruit upon all the available soil. Pine-apple growing has been largely extended in this island, as is now generally known at home; and as it is a source of some wealth to the colony, it may be incidentally mentioned in this running history of the place, and more particularly in reference to the fact that the Indian convicts upon ticket of leave have been often employed in its culture in order to earn a daily wage. The plant that produces the pine-apple known as the "ananas," or by the Malays as "nanas," grows literally wild upon the hills on Blakan Mati Island, and other islands round about Singapore. It delights in a moist climate, and here it has it to perfection, with just enough heat to help its growth. There is little or no trouble in its propagation, for after the apple is sufficiently ripe and cut, the crown that surmounts the fruit is planted, and a new plantation soon springs up. There is, however, some difference in the sweetness and flavour of the fruit, according to the exposure to which it is subjected, those having the benefit of the sun being preferred.

The first to export the tinned fruit to Europe was a Frenchman named Bastiani, who succeeded far beyond his expectations, and the industry has since been taken up largely by the Chinese in Singapore and Johore.

Yet another of the important public works of the colony, upon which the labour of Indian convicts was employed some five years earlier, was at the construction of the lighthouse on "Pedro Branca," called the "Horsburgh," after the celebrated hydrographer of that name. The design was by Thompson, and the selection of the site by Sir Edward Belcher, R.N., and most of the detail work was under the direct supervision of Mr. J. Bennett, a civil and mechanical engineer, who afterwards, as we have said, played a prominent part in the direction and control of the labour and industrial training of the Indian convicts in the Singapore jail. He had, as an assistant, Mr. Magaelhaens of the Convict Department, and both the officers and the convicts lived on board of a "Tonkong," or a large boat, which was anchored close to the rock. The convicts were chiefly employed in the capacity of blasters and dressers of stone. The foundation stone was laid with masonic honours by the Worshipful Master Brother M. F. Davidson, on the 24th May, 1850, in the presence of the Governor, Colonel Butterworth, and a large party from Singapore; and the work was completed and the lamps lighted on the 27th September, 1851.

The *Free Press* spoke of it as an edifice of which Singapore might well be proud. "The granite blocks which form the walls were quarried and shaped at Pulo Ubin, the timber used in the building was the growth of our island, the brass rails of the staircases were moulded and turned in this settlement, and last, not least, the architect and engineer acquired the skill and experience which enabled him to erect so rapidly the chaste and stately building during a long and useful career as Government Surveyor at Singapore." Both the quarrying of the stone at Pulo Ubin, and the felling of the timber required in the erection of this lighthouse, were by the work of Indian convicts.

In 1845 the foundation stone of a second lighthouse was laid on a reef near a small island at the eastern entrance to the Straits of Malacca called "The Coney." It was also laid with masonic honours by the Worshipful Master and Brethren of the Lodge Zetland in the East, No. 748, in the presence of the Governor, Colonel Butterworth, and many of the British and foreign residents at Singapore. This lighthouse was named after the eminent founder of the settlement, Sir T. Stamford Raffles, and was completed in 1856. It was built by free labour, but many convicts were employed, as at the "Horsburgh," as stone cutters, blasters, and as labourers, under the charge of an officer of the Convict Department.

We have referred elsewhere to the rules that had from time to time been framed for the control of these Indian convicts, but now we are able to state that in 1845-46 what may be called the most complete code of rules was permanently established. Colonel Butterworth, who was then Governor of the Straits Settlements, in consultation with the Superintendent of the Convicts, collected all that had been previously issued, together with those that subsequent experience had shown to be necessary, and working on the principles laid down by Sir Stamford Raffles, the new set of "Rules and Regulations for the Management of the Indian Convicts" was formally sanctioned, and put in force under the title of the "Butterworth Rules."

These rules practically recognised the total abolition of free warders in the control of the convicts, and the substitution entirely of petty officers, raised from amongst the convicts themselves, together with the division of the convicts into six distinct classes, according to their date of arrival in the prison, and their general subsequent behaviour; holding out to one and to all by exemplary conduct during their probationary period a certain progressive reward and promotion.

Added to these "Butterworth Rules" were several others of importance, introduced by Major McNair in 1858-59, and sanctioned by the Government from time to time as additions to this code. Later, Captain, now General, J. G. Forlong came to Singapore, as we have stated, to study the convict system in force; and from the rules in use and the numerous standing orders that had been issued at various times, he prepared a valuable digest of the whole, which he duly submitted to the Government of India, in which he said, "I have but lately visited most of the convict prisons of England, living for some time with the Governor of the Dartmoor jail, and I have seen many Indian prisons, and can state for the Singapore system and establishment, that it is not inferior to those of England, and quite unequalled by any I have seen in India."

It is to Captain, the late General, Man that the initiation of several handicrafts is due, and he commenced by starting all kinds of carpenter work. The old Guthrie's timber bridge across the Singapore River, for instance, was entirely their work. They were also then taught brick-laying and blacksmith work; and so valuable was this trained labour to the State, even at that time, that the Superintending Engineer of the station wrote to Government in 1849 as follows:—

"I can most confidently, and without fear of refutation, assert it to be simply impracticable to induce and obtain from Chinese carpenters that accurate, close, substantial, and lasting workmanship which not only can be, but is derived from the convict artificers under the absolute control of the present able and zealous Superintendent, Captain Man."

We must here not forget to refer to another public building, in the erection of which the Indian convicts took their part, viz. the New Civil Jail at Pearls Hill, the foundation stone of which was laid by Captain Faber, the Superintending Engineer of the Straits Settlements. Below the stone a brass plate was deposited with the following inscription, which we give in full as of some peculiar interest, and evidence of the progress of the settlement up to 1847.

This Foundation Stone
of
H. M. Gaol, at Singapore,
was laid by Captain Faber, Madras Engineers,
Superintending Engineer, Straits Settlements,
on the 6th February, 1847,
the 27th Anniversary of the Foundation
of a British Settlement
on this Island.
The Hon'ble Colonel W. J. Butterworth, C.B.,
being Governor of Prince of Wales Island,
Singapore, and Malacca,
and
the Hon'ble T. Church,
Resident Councillor at Singapore.
VICTORIA,
Queen of Great Britain and Ireland,
the Right Hon'ble Lord Hardinge, G.C.B.,
Governor-General of British India.
God save the Queen.

In a bottle, likewise placed below the stone, the following statistical information relative to the Straits Settlements, written on parchment, was enclosed.

The trade for the year 1845-46 of Prince of Wales Island, Singapore, and Malacca aggregated the sum of Company's Rs. 52,190,685 in merchandise, and Company's Rs. 9,606,061 in bullion and treasure, making a grand total of Rs. 61,796,746 (exclusive of the trade between the three settlements) as follows:—

		Imports.	Exports.		Total.
P.W. Island	Rs.	6,614,794	6,528,452	=	13,143,246
Singapore	"	26,616,448	21,162,987	=	47,779,435
Malacca	"	509,872	364,193	=	874,065

Grand total, Company's Rs.　61,796,746

W. J. BUTTERWORTH, GOVERNOR.

SINGAPORE, *6th February, 1847.*

The revenue and charges for the year 1845-46 of Prince of Wales Island, Singapore, and Malacca, including Civil, Military, Marine, Judicial, Convicts, etc., were as follows:—

Charges.

P.W. Island	Co.'s Rs.	402,783	15	11
Singapore	" "	497,186	14	5
Malacca	" "	231,158	12	5

	Rs.	1,131,129	10	5

Revenue.

P.W. Island	Co.'s Rs.	185,443	2	9
Singapore	" "	530,040	15	9
Malacca	" "	64,408	9	11

	Rs.	779,893	12	3
Total deficit at three settlements	Rs.	351,236	14	6

SINGAPORE, *6th February, 1847.*

In the year 1848 we find that the Indian convicts were employed in blasting some considerable part of a mass of rock known to the Malays as Batu Belayer, or "Stone to sail to," and by Europeans as "Lot's wife." It was a dangerous obstruction to navigation, being situated on the Singapore side of the western entrance to the New Harbour. It is reported as known to the old navigators of those seas, and was shown on old charts over two hundred years ago.

In following *The Anecdotal History* it may be well to mention here, as showing the steady progress of Singapore, that a census was again taken in 1849, which gave the total population at 59,043—Europeans being given at 198, Eurasians at 304, Chinese at 24,790; and the remainder was made up of Malays and other nationalities of the Indian Archipelago, and from the Coromandel Coast. This was recorded as only a trifling increase on 1848 amongst the Chinese, and was attributed to the decrease in the Chinese coolies working in the interior of the island, owing to the exhaustion of much soil, and the low price of produce, which had caused many of the planters to open new plantations in Johore.

As an evidence of the variety of the employments to which these Indian convicts were turned by the Government, it should be remarked that during the Chinese riots in 1851, when the Chinese Hwuys began to distrust their countrymen who had become converted to Christianity by a Roman Catholic mission in the interior of the island, these convicts were sent out in gangs to follow the rioters into the jungles and disperse them. These riots lasted for over a week, and it required the presence at last of the military to quell them. As it was, over 500 Chinese were killed, and among them many of the well-to-do Christian converts who had become planters.

Utilized as the services of these convicts from India were by the Government of that day, and their being wholly different in their habits, customs, and language from the Chinese who formed the bulk of the town population, it is not to be wondered at that the Chinese felt themselves estranged from them, and kept themselves ever aloof. There were, however, some Chinese of the lowest class who sought to embroil themselves with them, so as to bring the convicts into trouble, but the convicts always avoided a quarrel. They therefore sought other means, and in 1852 they gave out and placarded over the town that the Governor and all the Europeans had left worshipping in St. Andrew's Church, owing to the number of evil spirits there, and had gone to worship in the Court House, and that in order to appease the spirits the Governor required thirty heads, and had ordered the convicts to waylay people at night and kill them.

These placards created quite a panic in the place, so that people were for some days afraid to leave their houses after dark. In order to allay the fears of the people the Governor issued a proclamation saying that St. Andrew's Church had been struck by lightning and was unsafe (which was the fact), and he called upon the people not to believe the reports of evil men. Moreover, he offered a reward of $500 for the discovery of any person propagating such reports. This had no effect however, so the leading Chinese merchants were called upon to address their countrymen, which they did in a long appeal, assuring them of the benevolence of the Christian Government, and urging them to have no fear and not believe in foolish reports. In two days the fears of the Chinese population were thus dispelled. In 1875 a similar "head scare" occurred during the construction of the "puddle trench" for the new impounding reservoir. This was a work of considerable difficulty, and some superstitious natives circulated a report that it could not be done without "human sacrifice," and that the Government were looking for "heads" to put into the trench, and the alarm for days was so great that people would not pass along Thompson's Road adjoining the reservoir after dark; and even the "dhobies," or washer-men, in the stream adjoining the puddle trench, hastened into town before dusk. Similar so called "head scares" have occurred in Singapore up to even the present time. It is not easy to define what has led to this superstition in the native mind, and it is made more complicated from the fact that it is shared alike by Chinese and natives of India. In many of the Polynesian Islands the practice of human sacrifices we know exists even in our own days, and that chiefs, when they build a house or a war-canoe, offer up a human being; and the Polynesians and Indonesians resemble one another very closely. But such a superstition has not come to us through the Malay race, and we must rather seek for its origin from the Aryan Hindus of India; and as the Chinese took most of their tradition and folk-lore from the cradle of the Aryan races, the belief might thus be common to both peoples. The Rev. Mr. Ward, writing early in this century, refers to the human sacrifices at Bardwan, in Bengal, and says of them: "The discovery of murders in the name of religion was made by finding bodies with the heads cut off, and placed near the images of 'Durga' and 'Kali.'" Also at Serampur, before the temple of the goddess "Jara," a human body was found without a head. Whatever the origin of the superstition may be traced to, the municipality at Singapore were wisely advised, and we think very properly declined to take any notice of the recent "head scare" of this year, and we can only hope that these apprehensions will gradually cease to stir the minds of the people as they become more instructed and advanced in civilization.

Among the many works of utility carried on by convict labour during the tenure of the office of Superintendent of Convicts by Captain Man was the widening and improving of the Bukit Timah Canal, in order to drain the adjacent low lands, and render them capable for cultivation by market gardeners. In the cutting of these artificial channels the convicts from India had great aptitude, and some of them had been employed on similar work in their own country. The largest work, however, commenced in Captain Man's time, was the erection of the whole of the permanent buildings required for the location of the then large number of Indian convicts. They were built within the surrounding wall of the jail, near the "Brass Basa" or "Wet Rice" Canal, and entirely by the labour of the convicts themselves. The estimate for the work made by the Superintending Engineer for their execution by free labour was 100,000 rupees, but the money cost to the Government was only 12,000 rupees, when executed by convict labour and with convict-made materials. To effect this, the convicts were trained to make the bricks, to dig and burn coral for lime, to quarry stone for foundations, and to fell the timber in Government forests in the island, and to dress it for roof timbers, door and window frames, and so forth.

When Captain Man went to Malacca as Resident Councillor, Captain Ronald Macpherson, of the Madras Artillery, succeeded him as Superintendent of Convicts, Singapore, and carried on the works in progress at the time. This was in the year 1855. The most prominent work commenced by the convicts in his time, and subsequently carried to completion, was the erection of the new church, now the cathedral of the diocese. It must be acknowledged that it was a courageous act on the part of Captain Macpherson to have designed a church in the early English style of architecture, and to have pledged himself to the Government that he would undertake to construct it wholly by convict labour. We think it showed both confidence in himself and in his convict workpeople, and nothing could more clearly have proved to what perfection their skilled labour had advanced than that he felt himself able to embark on so elaborate a work.

It was in May of this year, 1855, that the Bengal Government approved of the project, and sanctioned the expenditure in cash of 47,000 rupees upon its construction. The Bishop of Calcutta laid the foundation stone during next year before a large concourse of the merchants and residents of the place, and the inscription below the stone ran as follows:—

The first English church of Singapore, commenced A.D. 1834, and consecrated A.D. 1838, having become dilapidated, this stone of a new and more commodious edifice, dedicated to the worship of Almighty God according to the rites and discipline of the Church of England, under the name of St. Andrew, was laid by the Right Reverend Daniel Wilson, D.D., Lord Bishop of Calcutta and Metropolitan, on the 4th March, 1856, in the twenty-fourth year of his episcopate.

The Hon'ble Edmund Augustus Blundell being the Governor of the Straits Settlements.

The Hon'ble Thomas Church being Resident Councillor of Singapore.

Lieut-Col. Charles Pooley, of the Madras Army, Commanding the Troops.

The Rev. William Topley Humphrey being Chaplain.

And Captain Ronald McPherson of the Madras Artillery being the Architect.

The Building to be erected at the charge of the Hon'ble East India Company.

Full Estimate of cost: Co.'s Rupees 120,932, or with Convict Labour Rupees 47,916.

In May, 1857, Captain Man proceeded from Malacca to Penang as Resident Councillor of that settlement, and Captain Macpherson took his place at Malacca. Captain Purvis, also of the Madras Artillery, was appointed to succeed Captain Macpherson in the combined duties of engineer and Superintendent of Convicts; but, to the regret of the Government, he relinquished the appointment at the close of the year, and Lieutenant McNair, another Madras Artillery officer, succeeded him. Lieutenant (now Major) McNair was a passed interpreter in the Hindustani language, which was spoken by the bulk of the convicts in the jail, and he subsequently qualified as a civil engineer. He remained in charge of the convicts until the jail was abolished in 1873.

Upon his assuming charge, the foundations of the new church had been laid and the masonry built up to nearly three feet above ground. The work was steadily carried on in accordance with the plans of Captain Macpherson, with the single exception that it was found necessary, owing to the weakness of the foundations, to abandon the heavy tower, and to place a light steeple instead. In the building of this church, Mr. John Bennett afforded most material assistance as Assistant Superintendent of Convicts. To his oversight and careful attention to the variety of details incident to such a work may be ascribed its satisfactory completion in January, 1862, when the edifice was consecrated by the then Bishop of Calcutta, Dr. George Cotton, who so unfortunately met his death in 1866 by being drowned in the Ganges. Further details in connection with this work will also be given under the heading of "Convict Industries and Public Works."

Footnotes:

He was known to both of us when he commenced the undertaking.

This entrance to Singapore was called New Harbour after the construction there of Cloughton's Dock, now the much improved New Harbour Dock. Singapore can now boast of another fine dock at Tanjong Pagar, constructed some forty years ago, and an additional dock is reported to be in contemplation.

The old mystic symbol of the Swastika of India, for instance, is common amongst the Mongolian races, and other signs of an early union between these races might be given.

Chapter VII

SINGAPORE (*Continued*)

To continue the narrative according to date, we trace that in the year 1858, after the mutiny, the Indian Government came to the conclusion that at all principal centres "field redoubts" should be constructed, to be available as places of refuge for Europeans in the event of a native rising; and accordingly orders were given for the fortification of Singapore. Colonel Collyer, of the Madras Engineers, was therefore sent over from Madras to design and carry out the necessary military works, and he was given the appointment of Chief Engineer of the Straits Settlements.

He selected Government Hill for the main work, and improved and enlarged the batteries on Mounts Palmer and Faber, being of opinion that, beyond the idea of a place of refuge, the island should be fortified to resist aggression from without. All his plans were approved, and, as Lord Canning had then become the first "Viceroy" of India, the main work was named after him, which name it bears to this day. In the execution of most of the earthwork, Chinese labour was employed, but the convicts were utilized in building the sally ports, constructing the drawbridge, sinking the deep wells; and the whole of the bricks, and much of the lime and cement required, were manufactured by the convicts at the Government kilns on the Serangoon Road. Colonel Collyer also designed other important works in the place, notably the Collyer Quay. Major Mayne, of the same corps, succeeded him, and in his time the waterworks scheme for the town was initiated, but not carried fully to completion, and fresh designs became necessary under his successor, in consultation with the late Sir Robert Rawlinson, K.C.B.

During this year also the convicts were employed in the erection of a new court house (now the public offices), the general hospital, lunatic asylum, pauper hospital, and some other minor public works. They also built the walls of the reclamation works along the sea front, now known as Collyer Quay, and above referred to, and the river wall at Campong Malacca. Both these sea and river works had been attempted by free labour, but the work of the convicts for this class of rubble walling was found more suitable, and therefore it was carried on by them, and with satisfactory results in every way.

View larger image

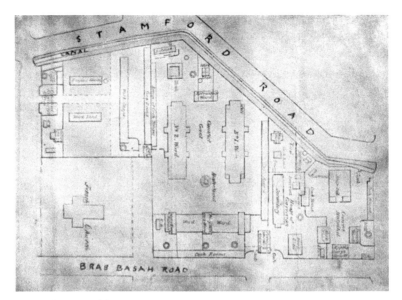

DISTRIBUTION OF JAIL BUILDINGS, SINGAPORE.

Plate X.

Shortly after the transfer of the Straits Settlements to the Crown, which occurred on the 1st April, 1867, the Governor, then Sir Harry St. George Ord, called upon Major McNair, who had been appointed Colonial Engineer and Comptroller of the Indian Convicts, to prepare plans for a Government House to be erected near Mount Sophia, somewhat under two miles from the town. The plans were approved by the Governor, and passed by the Legislative Council early in 1868. The land on which it stands cost $43,800, and the building, furniture, and laying out of the grounds, $115,000, and the work, with convict labour, was finished for the reception of H.R.H. the Duke of Edinburgh in December, 1869.

DESCRIPTION OF THE SINGAPORE CONVICT JAIL.

We have already incidentally referred to the plans of Captain Man for the erection of a permanent jail for the Indian convicts, which he had agreed to construct wholly by convict labour. The enclosure wall already existed, within which the original temporary buildings and thatched huts had been run up for their shelter. Only one solid building was within it, part of which was used as a hospital and the remainder for the confinement of convicts in irons. The next permanent building to be erected was quarters for the chief warder, and then came the solid gateways and guard-rooms. After these were built the wards for the fourth and fifth classes, or convicts in irons, then Nos. 1 and 2 wards, all shown on the plan (Plate X.) attached. Then a work-yard was enclosed by a solid wall, and offices built near the outer entrance to it, for the offices of the engineer and Superintendent of Convicts. While this wall was under construction by one gang, other gangs were employed in erecting within the main enclosure a refractory ward and punishment cells, and other minor buildings required in the way of store rooms, filter rooms, chain room, and a receiving room for fresh arrivals; and the effectual drainage of the whole prison.

It was only when all these buildings were actually completed, in the year 1860, that the establishment assumed the character of a prison; and the convicts themselves were not slow to realize the fact, for it became a proverb amongst them that "an open campong, or village, had become a closed cage."

MAIN GATE OF SINGAPORE JAIL.

Plate XI.

In 1857 there were altogether under the control of the convict authorities no fewer than 2,139 transported felons from India and about fifty from Hongkong. About one half of this number were localised in the main prison, the other half being employed upon the country roads, the quarries, and brickfields. These were of the third class; the second class men were detailed for duties as Government messengers, punkah pullers at the hospitals and Government offices, and others of this class also as "lookout men" at the flag-staff stations, helpers to light keepers, crews for the

Government boats conveying firewood to the jail and brick kilns, and others digging and conveying coral for lime burning.

In the main prison the wards were built of a uniform length of 230 feet, breadth 60 feet, and height of walls 20 feet. The wards were not ceiled, but open to the tiles, with a ridge ventilator along the whole roof. Beneath the side windows, which were barred, ground ventilation was provided, in order to ensure a current of air throughout the whole building. The floors were laid in concrete, and cemented over with "soorkee," or brick dust and cement mixed, and graded to the sides. Each ward was arranged to contain four hundred convicts. All the convicts were in association, separate confinement being restricted to the punishment cells. In each ward were platform sleeping benches. They were raised three feet at the head, and two feet nine inches at the foot, above the floor, and were coated with coal tar except on the actual sleeping place.

Lime-wash was used for the inner roofing timbers and tiles, and generally for the walls, except for the three feet of dado, which was coated with coal tar. Parts of this dado were daily re-coated with hot fresh tar, as we found coal tar to be a valuable deodorizer. To each ward there were four night urinals, detached from the main building and provided with double spring doors. In each urinal there were utensils coated with coal tar, and at every corner iron crates filled with wood-charcoal to absorb noxious vapours. Down the centre of each ward spit-boxes were provided for second and third class convicts accustomed to betel chewing. There was always a night watch of one petty convict officer in each ward, and surprise visits were often paid at night by the Superintendent, his assistant, and the chief warder. Going down a ward at night, one might see four hundred or more of these convicts, each enveloped from head to foot in a "chadar," or native sheet, literally over head and ears in sleep. They were all properly worked, properly fed, and properly punished when they deserved it; so, with the benefit of the two first, and a wholesome dread of the third, no wonder they were soon lulled to sleep when the prison doors were closed upon them. Now, at the risk of being a little tedious, we propose to describe in some detail the "day" latrines in use in this old jail. The information may, we think, be of service to those who have native prisoners under their charge either in jails or police stations in the East. At this period of time, when conservancy has rightly taken a first place in all such establishments, it may be thought by some to be superfluous, but the system pursued by us worked so very well that we do not hesitate to give an account of it.

There were many such latrines in the prison, so we will confine our remarks to one only. The building in use for this purpose was about seventy feet in length and twenty feet wide, and the tiled roof was supported upon brick pillars raised twelve feet from the ground. In its construction care was taken, above all things, to ensure a solid floor "impervious" to "moisture." This was made by first laying down six inches of well-prepared concrete, consisting of pounded granite, brick-dust, and gravel cemented together by hydraulic mortar, then overlaid with pure cement, and after this coated with an inch thick of asphalt. Around the whole building was an open drain, about two feet inside of the pillars, and built like the floor, and carefully graded to the outfall. The walls, pillars, and drains were coated with coal tar, and here and there daily renewed to ensure deodorization. Close to the drain, and at eighteen inches apart, were placed troughs of hard wood two feet in length, one foot nine inches wide, and nine inches deep, with stout handles at either end. These troughs were smeared over with pitch. Between every second trough was placed a box containing about a bushel of powdered red earth, perfectly dry, and in each box was a ladle made of half a cocoanut shell attached to a handle. Two convicts of the sixth, or feeble class, were placed in charge of this latrine, whose duty it was to see that the red earth was sprinkled by those using the troughs. When the troughs were full they were emptied into a conservancy cart with a hermetically closed screw top, and when this was full it was conveyed by bullocks to plantations in the country.

We think we are quite warranted in saying that this was the first jail, if not the first establishment anywhere, in which this dry earth system of conservancy was used. For centuries, no doubt, in India the well-known habit of the cat had been followed by many of the native castes, but it was not until vast numbers of these convicts from India were aggregated in association that the application of the system to their dwellings was initiated, and we think that the clever invention of the "earth closet" for certain localities may have suggested itself to its inventor when a resident at Singapore.

It may be as well to give here the testimony of Dr. Mouat, the Inspector-General of Jails, Bengal, on the efficiency of the conservancy of this old jail, and in no spirit of self-satisfaction we quote his own words "verbatim," which are as follows:—

"Singapore, *1st June, 1865.*—I have sincere pleasure in recording the unmixed satisfaction which I have experienced from a careful examination of the jail, and system of prison management in use at Singapore.

The scrupulous cleanliness, perfect plan of conservancy, excellent order, well-regulated system of labour and punishments, and the high standard of health attained are not surpassed in any other well-regulated institution of the same kind that I am acquainted with in Europe or in Asia. My personal knowledge of prisons and of all details of prison management is sufficiently extended to entitle me to speak with authority on this subject.

In many important points of internal economy and discipline, Singapore can fairly lay claim to being *Primus in Indis* in the adoption and practical working of principles that are now generally accepted as sound and correct. My own feeling on the subject is that Colonels Man and Macpherson and Captain McNair, to whom the chief credit appears to be due, are entitled to rank in the first class of prison officers and reformers in India."

Perhaps the last addition to the jail buildings was the erection by the convict bricklayers and plasterers of a stand to hold the prison bell, and from whence to call the roll at general musters. It was built in the form of a "monopteron," a sort of structure without walls, and composed of columns arranged in a circle, and supporting a covered cupola.

Footnotes:

Duke of Saxe-Coburg-Gotha.

These filters were of the simplest construction. They consisted of three very porous earthenware pots or "chatties" placed on a tripod. In the first was the water to be filtered, a foot off was the pot full of charcoal and white sand, and the filtered water was drawn off from the third. The charcoal and sand were renewed twice a week.

Chapter VIII

DIVISION INTO CLASSES, TRADES, FOOD, AND CLOTHING

We now come to deal with perhaps not a very inviting part of our subject, viz. the division of the convicts into classes, their supervision, artificer trades, hours of work, food, and clothing, but it must be told in brief in order to make the narrative of this jail complete.

They were divided into six classes, but since the year 1857, when Major McNair took charge, sec. A of the third class, and sec. A of the fifth class were added to the classification.

The *First Class* consisted of trustworthy convicts allowed out on ticket of leave.

Second Class consisted of convict petty officers, male and female, and those employed in hospitals and public offices.

Third Class were convicts employed on roads and public works, having passed through their probationary course.

Fourth Class were convicts newly arrived, and those degraded from other classes or promoted from the fifth class. They worked in light irons.

Fifth Class were convicts degraded from the higher classes, and such as required more than ordinary vigilance to prevent escape, or regarding whom special instructions had been received from India. They worked in heavy irons.

Sixth Class were invalids and superannuated convicts.

Youths were transferred to a special gang for "boys."

[Mcnair.

DUFFADAR RAM SINGH, SENIOR PETTY OFFICER OF THE JAIL.

Plate XII.

Convicts, if for life, were admitted to the first class after having been sixteen years in transportation; if for seventeen years, after twelve years; and if for seven years, after having been six years in transportation. Females, for whatever period, from three to five years. Before a ticket of leave could be granted, the convict had to provide personal security for his good behaviour and continued presence in the settlement; and any misdemeanour on his part involved a revoking of his ticket of leave, and his return to confinement in the prison and reduction to a lower class. All *First Class* convicts, whether male or female, had to attend muster on the first of every month, and had to keep the Superintendent informed of their place of residence, and were bound to sleep in it every night.

Second Class convicts were employed as stated. They were allowed to go out of the jail after working hours, but had to appear at 8 p.m. roll call daily (except those employed at hospitals and in special duties), and were required to sleep in prison at night. Convicts were admitted to this class, on good behaviour, at the Superintendent's discretion, as follows:—

If transported for 7 years, after 5 years.
"　　　　"　　14　"　　"　7　"
"　　　　"　　life,　"　8　"

All jail petty officers, from duffadars to orderlies, were included in this class, and no convict was eligible for an orderly until he had been eight years in transportation; promotion went either by seniority or qualification, but he should have been an orderly for two years before being promoted to a peon.

Third Class convicts. Convicts were admitted to this class at the Superintendent's discretion—

If transported for 12 years, after 12 months.
"　　　"　　14　"　　"　2 years.
"　　　"　　life,　"　3　"

This was not a chain class, and one rupee a month was allowed to each man for the purchase of condiments, called "subsistence money." If not belonging to the country gangs, and of approved good conduct, this class was allowed, after working hours, to be outside the prison until 6 p.m., if they had already completed four years in transportation; until that period had been discharged they were confined after work was over. This class was allowed to use their sectarian marks as a privilege. Degraded prisoners of this class were called "Sec. A, 3rd Class," and wore a ring on each ankle; they were strictly confined to the jail precincts.

**HEAD TINDAL MAISTRI OF CART MAKERS
AND WHEELWRIGHTS.**

Plate XIII.

Fourth Class. All newly arrived convicts, except those regarding whom special instructions had been received from India, were placed in this class, and served their probation in it. They were worked in double light irons, and were not allowed to leave the prison except for work; they were not granted any money allowance, but fish, vegetables and condiments were supplied to them with their rations. They were, however, allowed the privilege to cook their own food.

Fifth Class. This was a "punishment class" for troublesome characters from the upper classes, and every man degraded to it had to serve two years before being again promoted to the fourth class, and an additional six months before he could be promoted to the third class, unless the Superintendent saw sufficiently good cause for leniency. This class received clothing and rations like the fourth class, with vegetables, fish, and condiments; but all were cooked for them in mess under a convict cook. They received no money allowance, and were not allowed to leave the prison except for work. Refractory prisoners of this class were called "Sec. A, 5th Class"; they were put in the heaviest irons, with wrist irons if necessary, and were confined in the refractory ward on severe task work, as making coir from the rough husk of the cocoa-nuts, pounding and cleaning rice, and such like hard labour.

"Flogging": If upon rare occasions this punishment had to be resorted to, the culprit was first inspected by the medical officer to see if he were capable to undergo the sentence: usually the number of lashes was from one dozen up to six dozen with the cat-o'-nine-tails. If passed by the medical officer, the punishment was inflicted in the presence of the convicts, and by selected convict warders, the medical officer or his apothecary being invariably present during the infliction. The triangles were of the usual pattern, and the flogging was on the buttock.

No person was allowed to punish a convict but the Superintendent or the Assistant Superintendent acting for him. The defaulter was brought to the inquiry room, the case inquired into fully, and the default and sentence duly recorded in a book kept for the purpose.

CONVICT OF THE SECOND CLASS AND MUNSHI.

Plate XIV.

Sixth Class. This class embraced all invalid and incapable men who were able to perform light work, as sweepers, watchmen in country commands, and in charge of latrines; also caretakers at Government bungalows, and those superannuated men who were exempt from all work. No convicts were admitted to this class until declared unfit for hard work by the medical officer and the Annual Medical Committee. Men of approved conduct got the indulgences of their former class. Female convicts belonged to this class, of which there were always a few under transportation. They were confined in a separate ward under a convict matron, and no prison male warder was allowed therein on pain of degradation.

The supervising staff consisted of a Superintendent—who was also the Executive Engineer of the station—and his assistant, a chief warder and two assistants, an overseer of artificers and of roads. The native staff, being all petty officers raised from amongst the convicts, consisted of three duffadars, eight first tindals, twenty-two second tindals, ninety-four peons, and sixty-five orderlies, for the number of convicts then under confinement.

In the year 1857 there were 2,139 convicts from different parts of India, Burmah, and Ceylon in this jail; but upon an average, until the prison was broken up, there were 1,900 always under control. The men from India were Seikhs, Dogras, Pallis, or a shepherd race; Thugs and Dacoits from different parts of the Bengal presidency, and mostly from round about Delhi and Agra; felons from all parts of the Madras and Bombay presidencies, and a few from Assam and Burmah, chiefly Dacoits, and a sprinkling of Cingalese.

Upon arrival from India, each convict was checked with the warrants that accompanied the several gangs, then photographed, bathed, and supplied with the prison clothing, and each received a number by which, until he entered the third class, he was always known. Each convict was then duly inspected by the medical officer before admission to the wards. Any property with them was scheduled and put away until they were entitled to receive it, and the clothing in which they arrived was duly fumigated.

The artificer body was drawn from the third and fourth classes only, and they were subject to the same discipline as their classes in the general prison. They were divided into four grades, according to the degree of skill they evinced, and received a monthly allowance commencing at one half a rupee, or 1s. a month, up to the highest sum given to the best workmen of 10s. a month, who were called "tindal maistris," and who were entrusted with the duty of teaching beginners. These tindal maistris were exempted from keeping watch in the wards at night.

The several trades taught in the prison were as follows, and none of them were dangerous to health except the cement-sifting by females on treadles, which had to be discontinued:—

Bricklayers and plasterers.	Quarrymen.
Brick and tile makers and potters.	Sawyers, stone cutters, and blasters.

Blacksmiths.

Basket makers.

Coopers.

Carpenters, cement and lime burners.

Gardeners.

Painters.

Lime and charcoal burners.

Plumbers.

Slaters.

Shoe and sandal makers.

Tailors.

Turners and weavers.

Wheelwrights.

Woodcutters.

Boatmen.

Stone masons.

CONVICT OF THE FIFTH CLASS.

CONVICT OF THE FIFTH CLASS, SEC. A.

Plate XV.

Those few of the convicts who had acquired a trade in their native country were not admitted to the artificer gang until they had gone through their probationary period in irons on the public roads. The bulk of the convicts were trained in the prison itself; and after the year 1857 native methods of working were abandoned, and the use of our carpenter's bench introduced, and English tools employed in all trades.

They felled and stacked timber upon the island, which, after conveyance to the yard, was sawn and wrought into all that was required for roofing timbers, doors and window frames. They made the bricks, lime, and cement, and all tiles necessary for roofing or for paving. They quarried the stone at Pulo Obin for foundations, and for sea and river walls. The blacksmiths cast and forged from the raw state all the iron work for which there was a necessity. As a matter of fact all material and all labour for the execution of any public work required by the Government were executed by these convicts, from a small timber bridge upon a country road, even to the erection of a "cathedral" and "Government House," of which it is purposed further to give a detailed account.

This is the proper place in which we may mention that in the years 1859-60 the estimated value of this convict labour was 162,230 rupees, while the expenses of the whole convict department amounted to 117,578 rupees. In 1860-61 the manufacture account showed a balance of 25,028 rupees in favour of the State, though profit was always deemed of secondary importance. Material was valued at one half the market rate, and the labour at two-thirds the value of the same labour prevailing in the place.

The hours of work were limited to nine, including the time taken in marching to and fro from the works; but to add to discipline we would occasionally give them some extra hours of work, answering somewhat to our "pipebrooms" in the Navy, or the "pipe-claying of belts" in our Army on the line of march on active service.

CHETOO, AN INCORRIGIBLE CONVICT OF THE FIFTH CLASS.

Plate XVA.

The jail bell was rung at 5 a.m. (except Sunday), when every convict rose, rolled up his blanket with the number visible, and placed his "chadar" or sheet in his box, which was also numbered to correspond. He was marched out to the prison yard with the men of his ward, and the roll was called by the responsible officer. Time for light food was allowed, and the convicts were then detailed to the work gangs as arranged overnight. The work gangs left the prison punctually at 6 a.m., and returned at 11 a.m.; were marched out again at 1 p.m., returning at 5 p.m. At 6 p.m. a roll was again called for the 3rd, 4th, and 5th classes, who were then locked up for the night. At 8 p.m. there was another roll call for those who had the privilege, and then all were seen to their wards, and all wards and gates were locked by 9 p.m., when strict silence reigned throughout the prison; the European warder going rounds up to 10 p.m., and occasionally, with the Superintendent and his assistant, paying surprise night rounds. Convicts on the march out of prison were moved five abreast, or as they called it "pānch-pānch," literally, by "fives."

On the first of every month there was a general muster of the whole of the convicts, including the first class, when the roll was called, and each answered to his name or number. This muster was always in the presence of the Superintendent, who inspected each convict, and if any one had a grievance his name was taken down, and his complaint afterwards inquired into at the "Inquiry Room." This opportunity was taken by the Superintendent to inspect the whole prison, wards, latrines, drains, and bathing places.

The rations required for the jail were either obtained upon indent upon the Government Commissariat Department, or by tender called for in the town. Each convict's daily allowance was as follows:—

To 2nd, 3rd, and 6th classes without condiments.	Rice.	Dholl or Peas.	Salt.	Ghee, clarified Butter.	Vegetables.	Fish.	Mussala or Curr Stuff.
	oz.	oz.	drs.	drs.	oz.	oz.	drs.
Effective men	32	5	8	8	—	—	7¼
Invalids and Women	24	2	8	8	—	—	7¼

To the fourth and fifth classes, being effective, with condiments, fish and vegetables alternating thus—

	Rice.	Dholl.	Salt.	Ghee.	Vegetables.	Fish.	Mussalah or Curry Stuff.
	oz.	oz.	drs.	drs.	oz.	oz.	drs.
Monday	28	5	1	10	5	—	7¼
Tuesday	28	—	—	10	—	5	7¼

We found that this dietary scale was sufficient to a native under labour to repair waste tissue without giving fat. The "ghee," or clarified butter, made the rice more nutritious, and the "dholl," or peas, contained both albumen and starch, which would of themselves alone support life. For the penal class there was the usual congee diet.

All convicts not being in the first class, nor employed as messengers in hospitals or at public offices (when they received a compensation), were clothed in the jail.

The 2nd, 3rd, and 6th classes	—	—	Nine yards of stout grey shirting.
	—	—	One jail suit.
4th and 5th classes	half-yearly and duly marked		Two working suits and a stout cap.

To all annually was given one blanket of coarse wool called a "kumblie," and made by the convicts themselves from wool purchased in the place and prepared by them for the purpose.

Belts and brass plates for them were supplied only to duffadars, tindals, peons, and orderlies.

The European warders were dressed in a light blue serge loose coat with lace round the cap, and distinctive badge to indicate the grade, and in the case of an overseer of artificers a hammer and chisel crossed. After the reception in 1858-59 of a large number of mutineers they were supplied with a belt and revolver.

Chapter IX

PUBLIC WORKS AND INDUSTRIES

In referring to the variety of public works undertaken by these Indian convicts, we have hitherto refrained from going into much detail in regard to them; but we think it will not be without interest to dwell somewhat more at length, as we have proposed, upon the construction of the cathedral and the Government House, which still remain as records of their labour, and spring into the greatest prominence. Of the jail itself, which, as we have said, was planned and partially carried out by the late General Man, nothing further need, we think, be added for it is now dismantled except that it was in truth the training ground for the artificer gang under that able officer, who saw the absolute necessity of having some large public work in hand in order to the convicts acquiring a knowledge of the various trades. This principle in the management of convicts was advocated by Sir Edmund Du Cane in one of his pamphlets, in which he judiciously says that "the best system devised for the employment of convicts is that of executing large public works by means of their labour."

[*Koch.*

CATHEDRAL, SINGAPORE.

Plate XVI.

As the late General Man had for this purpose the erection of the permanent jail, so the late Colonel Macpherson planned and laid the foundations for execution by their labour of St. Andrew's Church, now the cathedral of the diocese; while to Major McNair fell the duty of designing and constructing almost wholly by these convicts the house for the Governor of the colony.

CATHEDRAL (see Plate XVI.).

In preparing the designs of this ecclesiastical edifice, Colonel Macpherson had to select as simple and easy a form of architecture as he could, and with as little ornament as possible, and therefore within the capacity of his workpeople; so he chose the Gothic, or rather, we should say, the Early English style of about the 12th century, and in so doing he said he had somewhat reproduced the character of old Netley Abbey. He laid the foundations, and saw it built up to about three feet above the ground, and then left for Malacca to take up the appointment of Chief Civil Officer there, and was therefore not able further to see the progress of the work that he had inspired. His plans, however, were carefully followed by his successor, with the exception, as has already been said, of substituting a spire for a tower, owing to undue settlement at the tower end. This building is 250 feet long internally, by 65 feet in width, with nave and side aisles; or, with the north and south transepts, 95 feet, the transepts being used as porticoes. The simple columns, with plain mouldings only, carried arches, on which rested the side walls of the nave, which were run up of sufficient height to clear the roofs of the aisles, and were perforated by a range of windows to admit light to the whole building. At the north-east end of the nave was a great arch leading into a chancel, and an apse with three lancet windows in stained glass. The building was roofed with teak timber, with a sarking of lighter wood as a lining to form a contrast, and then covered with slates imported from England. Over the main entrance is a vaulted dome, with a neat piece of groining in granite, also made by the convicts. Leading to the organ loft is a circular well staircase, made from quarter-inch plate iron, the treads and risers punched with holes by the punching machine in the work yard to render them lighter. They were bracketed together, and secured by screw bolts and nuts. The risers were bent round a two-inch bar of round iron, which passed down through all of them at the centre from top to bottom of the staircase. The whole was made and fixed in its place by the convicts.

As a pattern for the convicts to follow, we built two arches on the ground, the exact counterpart of those in the building; and, indeed, at any time when they wanted a guide, we had a model made; and the natives of India are such wonderful imitators, as we all know, that they soon were able to follow the copy we had given them. So the work progressed from day to day, until it was ultimately finished in 1862. We found that the skill of the convicts never failed them, and their capacity as builders and carpenters never seemed to slacken.

In dealing with the interior walls and columns, we used what is well known, though little employed with us in England, "Madras chunam," made from shell lime without sand; but with this lime we had whites of eggs and coarse sugar, or "jaggery," beaten together to form a sort of paste, and mixed with water in which the husks of cocoanuts had been steeped. The walls and columns were plastered with this composition, and, after a certain period for drying, were rubbed with rock crystal or rounded stone until they took a beautiful polish, being occasionally dusted with fine soapstone powder, and so leaving a remarkably smooth and glossy surface.

We have given the dimensions of this building, but we may remark that, owing to the simplicity of its tracery and mouldings, it really appears much larger than it actually is, and being built on an open space, its proportions at once strike the eye of every visitor to the colony.

A peal of bells was added to the cathedral in 1889 by the munificence of Mr. W. H. Read, C.M.G., who, with the late Mr. John Crawfurd, Mr. James Guthrie, and others, was instrumental in bringing about the transfer of these settlements to the Crown, and some of their portraits are now in the Town Hall, including that of Mr. Thomas Scott, then M.L.C.

MORTAR MILL, GOVERNMENT HOUSE, SINGAPORE.

GOVERNMENT HOUSE GARDEN BEING LAID OUT BY CONVICTS.

Plate XVII.

GOVERNMENT HOUSE (see Plate XIX.).

We have already mentioned that the transfer of the Straits Settlements from the direct control of India to the Crown was effected on the 1st April, 1867. The first Governor under the new *régime* was Colonel Sir Harry St. George Ord, R.E., who, upon his arrival in Singapore, had to take up his abode in a hired house. He therefore lost no time in issuing orders to purchase land, and to erect a suitable residence for himself and for the future Governors of the colony. Plans were accordingly called for from the colonial engineer (Major McNair), and they soon took shape and were submitted by the Governor to the Legislative Council without delay; and money was voted for the erection of the building, the purchase of land, and the ordering of furniture from England. The work was actually commenced within three months of the Governor's arrival, the foundation-stone was laid by Lady Ord a month later, and the building was made ready for the reception of H.R.H. the Duke of Edinburgh in October, 1869.

The whole of the brick work, exterior plastering, and most of the flooring and interior work were effected by convict labour; but it became necessary, towards the last, to employ free labour, to assist in the flooring, which was executed with battens from the steam sawmills at Johore, and also in the coffering of the ceilings in the drawing-room and some plastering in the rear block. The whole of the bricks used were made by the convicts, and much of the lime and cement was of their manufacture.

The edifice stands upon a hill in the eastern suburb of the town, about a mile and a quarter from the cathedral, and is surrounded by nearly 100 acres of ground, which has been tastefully laid out, and planted with rare plants under successive Superintendents of the Government Botanical Gardens. The building commands an extensive view of the harbour and surrounding country, and from the tower the distant islands and mainland of Johore are distinctly visible. It is supplied with water from the town water supply, by the use of a hydraulic ram. It was first lighted with gas, but now by the electric light throughout the whole building.

GOVERNMENT HOUSE, SINGAPORE, APPROACHING COMPLETION.

Plate XVIII.

The house is built somewhat in the shape of a cross. Ascending a flight of broad steps from the wide portico, you enter a spacious entrance hall floored with beautiful white marble from Java, having in your direct front a handsome stone staircase leading up through an arcade to a half-pace, from which it returns right and left to the lobby above, which is of the same dimensions as the entrance hall. Off this lobby, on the eastern wing, is the library, and beyond, the principal bed and dressing-rooms, and an open verandah over the portico (since regrettably built in). In the western wing is a double drawing-room, with disengaged pillars between; and below, off the entrance hall, on the east side, is the ball-room, and on the west the dining hall and billiard-rooms. Store-rooms, pantries, and all necessary accommodation were supplied as in any of our home mansions.

The ground floor of the building is raised four feet from the plateau, and ample ventilation is provided underneath. The building is 230 ft. in frontage, and 180 ft. in depth, and the height to the tower is 80 ft. The style is Ionic upon Doric, with Corinthian pillars and pilasters to the tower. It is roofed with slates, and the lower floors and verandahs are paved with marble.

As at the cathedral training for the convicts, so here models of the pillars and capitals were made on the ground for them to copy, and the special bricks for mouldings, copings, architraves, and capitals were made at the convict brick kilns. The plaster work for the exterior walls was a subject of much consideration with us; and, after various experiments, we arrived at the following composition, and it has thoroughly withstood the weather, which, under the trying circumstances of a rapid succession of damp and heat, was exceptional in that climate:—

Portland cement	2 parts.	
White selected sand	1 part.	Carefully and slowly mixed by the convicts.
Granite powdered to dust in small handmills, or querns	— 2 parts.	

A gift by the Chinese community of a statue of H.M. the Queen was unveiled with some ceremony at this Government House in the year 1889.

INDUSTRIES (INTRA-MURAL).

We have already enumerated the various trades that were taught to these Indian convicts, and shall therefore confine our remarks here to a brief description of some of those productive occupations upon which we employed their labour both within and without the main jail.

We must, however, make known beforehand, in connection with intra-mural works, that, attached to the main jail, yet distinctly separated from it by high walls and a guarded gateway, was a "work-yard," in which were built shops for carpenters, blacksmiths, coopers, wheelwrights, sawyers, stone-cutters, and turners in wood and iron.

[McNair.

GOVERNMENT HOUSE, SINGAPORE, COMPLETED.

Plate XIX.

In one part of this yard was also a machine shop, in which were fitted lathes, punching and shearing machines, and a bolt and nut machine, also a band saw and a circular saw table. To drive this machinery a 12 h.p. engine was used, and this was placed under the charge of a convict who had been employed in the engine-room of a P. and O. steamer, and had gone through his probationary period in the jail. Added to these machines was one of Blake's stone-crushers to break stone of various gauges for metalling the roads of the town.

This was the first Indian jail, and we might even go so far as to say it was amongst the first of any jails, where convicts were employed in connection with steam power. We had, it is true, an engine to be worked by manual power, for six or eight men abreast, to drive the circular saw, but it did not answer. It was intended as "crank" labour for the convicts.

When Dr. Mouat, the Inspector-General of Jails, Bengal, wrote his annual report of 1864-65, he said: "I have suggested the introduction of steam machinery for the spinning of jute yarn, in order that all prisoners sentenced to rigorous imprisonment may never be without the hard labour which the jail is bound to provide for them. In this, as in most matters connected with the organization of prison industry, I have been anticipated by the authorities at Singapore, there being a steam saw-mill in use at the Singapore jail, and a pug-mill employed in the preparation of the clay used in the brick and tile manufactory."

The carpenters made every necessary article required for the public buildings in progress; even the pulpit, reading-desk, and interior fittings for the cathedral were the work of their hands. The blacksmiths had four smithies, and forged, cast, and prepared all kinds of ordinary iron work found necessary. The coopers made buckets, tubs, and all the casks for storing cement, and for other jail purposes. The wheelwrights made all the carts, barrows (hand and wheel), and the hack-barrows wanted at the brick kilns. The stone-cutters turned out the mouldings, mullions, capitals, cills, steps, and all that was essential in our building operations.

Within the jail proper there were shops for tailors, weavers, rattan workers, coir and rope makers, flag makers, a printing press, and a photographic studio, and a few draughtsmen for executing plans and working drawings. The tailors cut out, made, and repaired the clothing for the fourth and fifth classes, and any other such occupation required in the prison. The weavers, who worked with an ordinary Indian hand-loom, made the coarse cloth required for those classes in irons, and washed, dressed, combed, carded, and spun the raw wool purchased from the butchers in the town, from which the "kumblies" or coarse blankets supplied to all the convicts were made. The coir or yarn manufactured from the husks of cocoanuts was prepared by those employed at "hard labour" in the refractory ward. From this yarn we made cordage for the convict boats, mattresses for the hospitals, and matting of various kinds. The flag makers made up and repaired the flags and colours for the signal stations, and for the department of the master attendant. Upon this work female convicts, and feeble men of the sixth class, were usually employed.

The printing press was established in 1860, and to start it the services of a Portuguese foreman printer were engaged for a short time to teach the convicts; and bookbinding was added later on. Photography was taught by one of us to two intelligent convicts of the Calcutta Baboo class who wrote English. All convicts had their likeness taken, and were registered for identification in case of escape; also local prisoners and men under custody by the police. We had not, of course, the knowledge then of Mr. Henry's method of identity by means of "finger-prints," for it was only approved last year by the Government of India. The draughtsmen, numbering three, executed all the plans and working drawings for the public works. Those for the cathedral and Government House, and many other buildings, were drawn by these men, the principal draughtsman being a convict transported from Bombay of the name of Babajee. The rattan workers wrought chairs and baskets of all kinds, fenders for the Government steamers, and signal baskets for the flagstaff's.

There were other minor industries carried on within the prison walls, so that it was a busy scene of task work from one end to the other, for every one was engaged upon something, and there was no chance for an idler to do nothing. Nursing a job was quite out of the question.

But we must pass on to deal with the industries beyond the walls, and we shall limit our description to the making of bricks, lime, and cement, and the quarrying of stone, and well digging.

INDUSTRIES (EXTRA-MURAL).

It will be quite superfluous to give an account in detail of the method pursued in brick and tile making, for the process is known to every one. Suffice it to say that Colonel Faber, R.E., as previously noted, was the first to introduce the manufacture on Government account; he opened a place at Rochore, near the present gasworks, and employed free labour. The system was what is known as the "dry" and sand-moulding system, and the bricks were burned in clamps. All that could be said of these bricks was that they were better than those made by the Chinese at that time, but they were not a success, and the manufacture was after two or three years given up.

In 1858 we started, on a systematic principle, under a trained European brick maker, an extensive brick field on the Serangoon Road, about three miles from the town, where there was a considerable bed of excellent clay for the purpose. The site, too, was well situated near the banks of an inlet from the sea, and affording great facility for water carriage, and with a palm grove close at hand, under the shade of which the convicts were allowed to roam without restraint when their work was over. Sheds, kilns, pug-mills, moulding tables, and all the necessary appliances for hand-made bricks were soon set on foot, and a large dormitory, surrounded by a stout precinct fence, was built for the number of convicts required for the manufacture, approximating to about 120 of all classes, except those in irons.

Our process was commonly known as "slop-moulding," each moulder turning out from 2,500 to 3,000 bricks in the course of the day. After the second year, when the convicts had become accustomed to the work, and to adapt themselves to each other, we were able to supply all that were needed for the public works, and even to export them for works at Malacca. In tabulating the account of the value of their labour and the outlay for fuel, and comparing it with the recognised value of the bricks, there was found to be a credit to the State in most years. (See Appendix No. 4.)

When, in 1867, there was an Agricultural Exhibition at Agra, in the N.W. Provinces of India, we sent up specimens of bricks, tiles, drain pipes of all sizes, and stable flooring bricks, manufactured by these convicts, for which the Superintendent gained the silver medal; and if any further proof is needed of the excellent work turned out by these convicts, we may quote the report of the late Colonel Fraser, of the Bengal Engineers, which ran as follows:—

"As an Engineer Officer of the D.P.W., I have had a good deal of experience as regards the management of jails in India and Burmah, and have, of course, employed much convict labour, but I have never been in any jail where the arrangements are so perfect as in that of Singapore. While the discipline under which the convicts are held is obviously most efficient, the skill with which their labour is directed will be equally obvious to all who will take the trouble, as I have done, to go into the detail of their operations, and look at the results in the many large works which have been executed at Singapore.

I went over the brick field with Captain McNair, and while I found that the greatest reasonable amount of work was got out of each man, I also found that the work turned out was the best I have seen in India. Where there are good bricks, other work is seen to be equally good, and when a proper amount of work is required per convict, then the discipline must be also good; I measured myself what the men were expected to do, and found it to be three cubic yards in eight hours. This is the full task of a European sapper in the same time."

CONVICTS STONE-QUARRYING, AT PULO OBIN, SINGAPORE.

Plate XX.

Our lime and cement were made from coral, of which there were extensive reefs round the Island of Singapore, and some few "atolls" (a Cingalese word), or special coral islands. Coral is almost a pure carbonate of lime, and therefore very well suited for the purpose. It was broken up and heated in kilns constructed for the purpose. The cement was made from this lime, and from selected clay, in the proportions we had by careful experiments established, until we obtained a good and quick-setting article. It was made into small balls and then dried, and burnt in a special kiln, and afterwards well and finely ground and sifted by female convicts; its tensile strength was excellent.

STONE QUARRYING (see Plate XX.).

The stone we used for all our building operations was procured from an island between Singapore East and the mainland of Johore, and was named Pulo Obin. It is about three miles long and three-quarters of a mile broad. The stone was the best possible form of crystallised granite, fine grained, very compact and durable, grey in colour, with here and there black patches or nodules of hornblende. It occurs in large fluted boulders, and was wrought by the convicts by fire, or by blasting with gun-powder, or split by pointed chisels and large hammers. Its weight was 168 lbs. per cubic foot. The excellent quality of this granite led the Government of India to approve of the construction by the late Colonel Eraser, C.B., of several courses for the Alguada Reef lighthouse, which was built upon a dangerous reef off the coast of Burmah. Our department looked after the preparation of some of these courses, and forwarded them by ship to Burmah.

WELL DIGGING.

It is known to everyone how capable the Indians are in the sinking of wells, and that with many Orientals it is a work of great merit to build one. As two were required for Fort Canning, we were soon able to select men fitted for this special work amongst the third class convicts, who, many of them, begged to be allowed to take part in their construction. After a careful set of borings, we came upon water at a depth of 180 and 120 feet respectively. They were eventually dug out to these depths, and steined to six feet in diameter by the use of sound and hard bricks from the convict kilns. The water rose to a height of 80 feet from the surface of the ground, and they were provided with lift and force pumps for the convenience of the troops in garrison. It was a heavy job for the convicts, but they performed it with eagerness and alacrity.

Footnotes:

Archdeacon and Chaplain, Ven. John Perham;

Choirmaster, Mr. C. B. Buckley; |– 1899.

Organist, Mr. E. Salzmann.

Colonel Macpherson had seen as a young man the ruins of the old church and abbey of Netley, or "Letley," as it was originally called, from the Latin word "lætus," pleasant, and the Saxon word "ley," a field, and had been so impressed with the simple character and proportions of the Early English style of church architecture, of which this was an excellent example, that when called upon to plan a new church for Singapore, he, as we say, chose this as his model.

We have a very good account of Netley Abbey given in 1848 by George Guillaume, architect, and from his description it was founded in 1239, and was occupied by monks of the Cistercian order, who were brought over from a neighbouring monastery at Beaulieu in the New Forest, where there was already an abbey dedicated to the Virgin Mary. Netley Church was built on a cruciform plan, and was proportioned according to the ancient mysterious figure called the "Visica Pisces," as will be seen in the sketch below from his work.

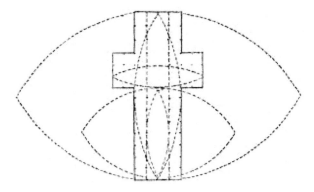

Singapore Church, now, as we have said, the cathedral of the diocese, has been much admired for its true symmetry and exact proportion, as well as for the delicate simplicity of its details.

Also a work which we initiated and brought to completion on designs approved by the late Sir Robert Rawlinson, K.C.B.

All taught by ourselves to the convicts, with the assistance of Overseer Callcott, now risen to be Deputy Colonial Engineer.

Major McNair, who himself supplied both apparatus and chemicals.

Chapter X

STORIES ABOUT INDIAN CONVICTS AND EUROPEAN LOCAL PRISONERS

No. 1

Most of the convicts sentenced to the Straits Settlements for short periods of transportation were, as we have said, usually retained in the convict jail at Malacca. Amongst these, in the sixties, was a very remarkable man, and known to both of us, of the name of "Tickery Banda," who was a native of Ceylon, and had received a sentence of seven years in transportation for a crime committed in that island, though of which he declared, like many of his congeners, he was perfectly innocent.

A story in connection with this man is given in Cameron's *Tropical Possessions in Malayan India*, which is quite worthy of repetition here.

When the English took possession of Kandy, Tickery Banda and two or three brothers, children of the first minister of the King of the Kandians, were taken and educated in English by the then Governor of the island. Tickery afterwards became manager of some coffee plantations, and was so employed on the arrival of a Siamese mission of priests in 1845, who came to see Buddha's tooth. It seems that he met the mission returning disconsolate, having spent some 5,000 rupees in presents and bribes in a vain endeavour to obtain a sight of the relic. Tickery learned their whole story, and at once ordered them to unload their carts and wait for three days longer, and that he would in due time obtain for them the desired view of the holy tooth. He had a cheque on a bank for £200 in his hands at the time, and this he offered to leave with the priests as a guarantee that he would fulfil his promise. He did not say whether the cheque was his own or his master's, or whether it was handed over or not; perhaps it was this cheque for the misappropriation of which he found his way to the convict lines of Malacca. The Siamese priests accepted his undertaking and unloaded their baggage, agreeing to wait for the three days. Tickery immediately placed himself in communication with the then Governor, and represented, as he says, forcibly, the impositions that must have been practised upon the King of Siam's holy mission, when they had expended all their gifts and had not yet obtained the desired view of the tooth. The Governor, who, Tickery says, was a great friend of his, appreciated the hardships of the priests, and agreed that the relic should be shown to them with as little delay as possible. It happened, however, that the keys of the temple where the relic was preserved were in the keeping of the then Resident Councillor, who was away some eight miles elephant shooting. But this difficulty was not long allowed to remain in the way, for Tickery immediately suggested that it was very improbable that the Resident Councillor would have included these keys in his hunting kit, and insisted that they must be in the Councillor's house. He therefore asked the Governor's leave to call upon Mrs. ——, the Resident Councillor's wife, and, presenting the Governor's compliments, to request that a search be made for the keys. Tickery was deputed accordingly, and by dint of his characteristic tact and force of language, carried the keys triumphantly to the Governor.

The Kandy priests were immediately notified that their presence was desired, as it was intended to exhibit the great relic, and that their guardian officer would be necessary. Accordingly, on the third day, the temple was opened, and in the building the Siamese priests and worshippers were assembled, with Tickery on the one side, and the Kandy or guardian priests on the other side, with the Governor and the Recorder in the centre.

After making all due offerings to the tooth of the great Buddha, the Siamese head priest, who had brought a golden jar filled with otto of roses, desired to have a small piece of cotton with some of the otto rubbed on the tooth, and then passed into the golden jar, thereby to consecrate the whole of the contents. To this process the Kandy priests objected, as being a liberty too great to be extended to foreigners. The Siamese priests, however, persisted in their request; and the Governor and Recorder, not knowing the cause of the altercation, asked Tickery to explain. Tickery, who had fairly espoused the cause of the Siamese, though knowing that in their request they had exceeded all precedent, resolved quietly to gratify their wish; so, in answer to the Governor's interrogatory, he took from the hands of the Siamese head priest a small piece of cotton and the golden jar of the volatile oil. "This is what they want, your Honour: they want to take this small piece of cotton, so—; and having dipped it in this oil, so—, they wish to rub it on the sacred tooth, so—; and having done this, to return it to the golden jar, so; thereby, your Honour, to consecrate the whole of the contents of the golden jar."

All the words of Tickery were accompanied by the corresponding action, and of course the desired ceremony had been performed in affording explanation. The whole thing was the work of a moment, and the Governor and Recorder did not know how to interfere in time, though they knew also that such a proceeding was against all precedent. The Kandy priests were quite taken aback, while the Siamese priests, having obtained their desired object, took from Tickery Banda's hands the now consecrated golden jar with every demonstration of fervent gratitude. The Kandy priests were, however, loud in their indignation, and subsequently the Governor, patting Tickery on the back, said, "You have indeed settled the question, and it is a pity you were not born in the precincts of St. James', for you would have made a splendid political agent."

The next morning Tickery received a douceur of 1,000 rupees from the Siamese priests, and has ever since been held in the highest esteem and respect by the King of Siam and his Buddhist priests, being considered quite a holy man, while periodically the King of Siam sends him substantial tokens of the Royal favour.

*   *   *   *   *

No. 2

It was remarkable what a wide difference there was between the accounts given by the convicts themselves, of the circumstances which were the cause of their transportation, and the summary of them given in the warrants sent with them. Although many of them did not deny having committed what the law looked upon as a crime, they, under the circumstances, either considered that the act was justifiable, or perhaps that it was the result of accident. Here is the case of a convict who was sentenced to transportation for life for murder, given as related by himself.

"In my Madras native village, I 'Rudrapah' was a planter (ryot). I was possessed of several large paddy fields; some were near my house and others were far off. At a little distance from my house a friend of mine lived, 'Allagappen' by name. He also was a ryot, and possessed of paddy fields. He often came to eat rice with me, and I often went to his house; we were like brothers. At a village about six miles away, there lived a man who was a breeder of cattle. He and his wife were very partial to me, and it was arranged between us that I should marry their daughter when she was old enough—she was then eleven years of age. All went well for two years, and then I was married to the girl and took her to my house. My friend, 'Allagappen,' used to come and visit us and eat rice as before. Things went on very well for five or six years: my wife and I were very happy together, and never quarrelled; we had only one child. Having saved some money, I bought a bandy (a country vehicle) and a pair of bulls, and used to hire them to any one travelling. Sometimes my bandy would be engaged for a long journey, and I would be away from my house for two or three days together, leaving my wife and child alone. But now my trouble began. About six months after I bought my bulls, one of them got sick and died. I had not then enough money to buy another, and was on the point of selling the bandy and remaining bull, when my wife proposed that we should ask her father to help us, as he had plenty of bulls. I had not thought of this, and I said, 'Very good.' We went and saw my father-in-law, and he agreed to let me have a bull and pay for it as I earned money. Soon after that I hired my bandy to a man to go to a town thirty miles away, expecting to be away some days. I left my wife and child under the charge of a neighbour and his wife, who promised to look after them. I and the man who hired my bandy set out early in the morning, and reached the town about mid-day next day. In the evening the man told me he was going to stay many days in the town, and I could return to my house. He paid me, and I bought some things I wanted. Early next morning, at daybreak, I set out on my journey back to my village, and arrived there about 3 o'clock the next morning; and after seeing to my bulls I went to my house and to my surprise found the door unfastened. I entered without making any noise, not knowing what could be the reason the door was not fastened. I went quickly into my sleeping place, and there I saw my wife laying asleep, and beside her was a man also asleep. On going close up to him that I might see who it was, to my great sorrow I found that it was my friend, 'Allagappen.' It was my great misfortune that I had in my hands a granite stone, or sort of muller, for grinding massalah (curry stuff) which I had bought, and being so angered with my friend, and so overcome with grief at finding my wife to be false, it made me tremble so much that I let the stone fall from my hands, and quite unintentionally it dropped on 'Allagappen's' head, and the stone being heavy it broke his skull and killed him on the spot. My wife woke up, and seeing me, she screamed and ran away from the house. She went to the neighbours' house in whose charge I had left her. I followed her, and told them what I had done: that morning I was taken by the police and locked up, and after that I saw my house no more. I was tried by an English judge, and was sentenced to be sent away from my country for as long as I lived: such was my misfortune."

Here the tears came into the old criminal's eyes, and it was very evident that there was still a soft place in his heart, showing a sign of reclamation in spite of his convict life. This convict was pardoned after serving twenty-five years.

*　　*　　*　　*　　*

No. 3

As late as the year 1863 piracy had not been wholly suppressed in the Straits of Malacca, and cases were by no means rare of native trading craft being attacked by them. During this year a number of piratical boats infested the mouths of the rivers Prye, Juroo, and Junjong on the Malay Peninsula, and the South Channel between Penang Island and the mainland of Province Wellesley; and many a tongkong belonging to Chinese traders between Penang and Laroot was attacked by them and plundered, and sometimes the crews were murdered.

Some of these pirates were in the habit of going about in Penang and quietly ascertaining what tongkongs were about to sail, and all particulars in regard to their cargo, crew, and so forth. Two of them having discovered that a tongkong owned and manned by Chinese was about to leave Penang for Laroot with some valuable cargo and $2,000 of specie on board, disguised themselves as "hadjis," or Mohammedan pilgrims, and engaged a passage in her. They arranged with some of their confederates to have a prahu, or fast sailing boat, at a certain place off the Juroo River, and when the tongkong in which they were passengers reached this spot a signal was to be given, and the prahu was to run alongside the tongkong; and after plundering her and gagging the crew, the pirates intended sinking the tongkong and making off in the prahu. They carried their villainous scheme into execution, but meeting with stouter resistance from the crew of the tongkong than they had anticipated, they killed, as they thought, every man on board, and were preparing to scuttle the tong-kong, when a boat containing Indian convicts, and employed in carrying coral for the Government lime kilns, and which, unperceived by the pirates, had been rapidly approaching, came alongside the tongkong, having been attracted by the yells and cries of the victims. The pirates, recognizing that they were convicts, immediately got into their prahu, and made sail as fast as they could; and she, being a very fast sailer, was soon out of sight. The convict tindal in charge of the boat, with one or two convict boatmen, went on board the tongkong and found all the crew and passengers dead; but fancying they heard groans they searched round the tongkong, and at last found one of the Chinese boatmen clinging to the rudder. They lifted him on board, and found that he was severely cut about, and covered with wounds. The convict tindal in charge of the Government boat then shaped his course, with the tongkong in tow, for Butterworth, in Province Wellesley, which they reached early in the morning. The wounded Chinaman was taken to the hospital, a report was made to the police of the pirates' attack, and the tongkong was handed over to their charge. From the description of the prahu given by the convict tindal, and the information gathered from the Chinaman when he was able to talk, the police were enabled to trace the prahu to Sunghie Rambay, where the pirates were arrested. The case was tried at the Supreme Court, Penang; some of the pirates were hanged, and the rest sentenced to penal servitude. The tindal of the Government boat and the convict boatmen were highly commended by the judge for their conduct, and were otherwise rewarded by the authorities.

*   *   *   *   *

We have referred elsewhere to the numerous races of India which went to form the convict body in the old Singapore jail. We found this admixture of castes and tribes a very valuable corrective against a possible chance of insurrection, and for the discovery of plots of escape; and, indeed, sometimes as a means of finding out any serious mischief that might be brewing in the jail.

It seems to delight many a native of India to be a spy upon another; and though intrigues were never encouraged, nor as a rule listened to, yet now and again an informer would appear when the matter was of sufficient importance to be reported to the authorities.

As an instance of this it may be recorded that on one occasion there was a dispute between two Sikhs, one of the "Ramdasee" and the other of the "Mazahbee" sect; and as they went from high words to blows they were placed in confinement and brought before the Superintendent in the Inquiry room. After full investigation into the matter, the "Mazahbee" Sikh was proved to have been the instigator of the quarrel, and he was punished. The whole of his sect appear to have resented this judgment, and determined amongst themselves to be avenged, and to inflict some pain or injury upon the Superintendent. They began to plot and to scheme as to the best way to carry out their design; and this plotting was not lost on the observation of a clever Parsee convict, who, having traded in Northern India, knew their language. He watched them closely, and had decided when their plans were matured to inform the authorities.

The scheme was only ripe for execution, however, on the very morning of the muster, so that there was no time for the Parsee convict to acquaint the chief warder; and as a last resource, therefore, he made up his mind to inform the Superintendent at the muster as to what was in store for him. Creeping stealthily along the rear of the standing men, he timed the arrival of the Superintendent going down the front on his inspection; and, stooping down, he thrust his head between the legs of the front rank men, and level with the ground, calling out only loud enough for the Superintendent to hear, "Khabardar sahib Sikh kepas tamancha hai"— "Look out, sir; a Sikh has a pistol." The Superintendent took no notice of the warning until he had passed to about the middle of that line, then he ordered the chief warder to take a dozen of the Sikhs who were standing at the end of the line, and move them off into their ward that he might inspect their boxes, and he added, "Search them thoroughly."

As the Superintendent passed the end of the line, and was about to inspect another line at right angles to it, no shot had been fired; so he concluded that it was either a false alarm, or that the miscreant was amongst the dozen men in the ward. And so it proved; for shortly afterwards, the chief warder came to report that he had found a loaded pistol on the person of one of the Sikh convicts, and had placed him in a cell to await investigation.

After the muster an inquiry accordingly took place, and it turned out that a fellow-tribesman had managed to pass the main gate with a pistol secreted about his person, and had handed it to the man to whom the lot had fallen to do the deed.

The would-be assassin was sentenced to heavy irons, and placed in the refractory ward. The gang was eventually broken up, the ringleaders being transferred to Penang, and the remainder kept in Singapore under close observation. The Parsee convict, who checkmated the conspirators, was advanced from the third to the second class, and otherwise rewarded.

The design on the life of the late Colonel Macpherson, the immediate predecessor of the above, was also similarly frustrated by another Parsee, who, on the evening before muster, observed a man burying a knife in the sandy ground near which he had to stand for inspection. Waiting his opportunity, he proceeded to the spot and withdrew the blade from the knife, and replaced the handle just above the ground as he had found it. When Colonel Macpherson passed the man on the morrow he quickly seized the handle from the ground to make his stab, but only to find that he was unexpectedly baulked in his villainous attempt to kill his Superintendent.

∗   ∗   ∗   ∗   ∗

No. 5

"FUNNY JOE"

His surname need not be mentioned, but he went by the name of "Funny Joe." He was the son of a clergyman of the Church of England, sharp witted, and well educated; but his moral character, from some cause or another, became quite disorganised, and to the grief of his parents he left his home and took to the sea. His education there stood him in good stead, and under new surroundings he improved for the time, and eventually rose to be chief mate of a ship. Had he persevered in this good course, he would in all probability have succeeded well in the mercantile service; but events proved otherwise, and on his second voyage as mate he was, he said, wrongfully charged as being both insolent and insubordinate to his commander, and on the arrival of the vessel at the Cape of Good Hope he was discharged. Left with but small means, and, to him, almost on foreign soil, he bethought himself of some expedient for making money; so, getting hold of a sailor loafing at the port, he talked matters over with him, and they decided upon clubbing their resources, hiring a hall, and circulating posters that on a certain night at "so much," and "so much" for entrance, a man might be seen "walking on the ceiling like a fly." On the night advertised the hall was crowded. "Funny Joe" then went to his companion, who was collecting the money, and took from him the amount he had received, and told him he might have all the rest that he could collect. He (Funny Joe) then decamped, and was never heard of more in Cape Town. He was next at Rangoon, where he got into the same plight for want of funds; but his mother wit came to his aid again, and this time he posed before the public as a naturalist who had discovered off the coast what he pronounced could be nothing else than a "mermaid," and for the exhibition of this marine creature, which he had cleverly constructed from the head and breast of an ape and half the body of a fish, he obtained a good round sum. We hear of him next at Singapore, where he also advertised his "mermaid" as being on exhibition at a certain boarding establishment. There, however, the "mermaid" did not succeed, and his funds being exhausted he possessed himself of a watch and some cash, the property of the people of the house with whom he lodged, and for which he was sent to jail. Here he came under some strict discipline and good wholesome advice, and it was in the Singapore jail that he told the story of his life as given above.

When the term of his sentence had expired, and he was about to be discharged, he warmly thanked the Superintendent for his counsel, and declared very positively that he intended to turn over a new leaf.

We believe that he did so; at all events, the last heard of him was that he had signed articles as mate of a ship; and he scrupulously returned to the Superintendent (Major McNair) the money he had advanced to him from his private purse to make a new start in life.

*   *   *   *   *

No. 6

CONVICTS WITH A COBRA AND A CROCODILE

It is well known that the Cobra di Capello is one of the most deadly of the snakes of India and the East. The palish yellow cobra of India is perhaps more dangerous and surely fatal in its bite than the black "cobra" or "kala samp," which is more frequently found in the Straits Settlements, but neither of them is very pleasant to be in close proximity to.

The Cobra.—As we have noticed elsewhere, some of the convicts were very expert in catching these reptiles and extracting their fangs. The following personal incident is given by a public works officer:—

"When the new cantonments were in progress at Tanglin I was placed in charge of the works by Col. G. C. Collyer, R.E., the then Chief Engineer of the Straits Settlements, and was permitted to occupy a part of a large house on the estate. The bath rooms were on the ground floor, and stairs from the bedrooms above led down to them. One morning, just as I was sitting down to breakfast, my convict orderly came running to me and said that a large 'cobra' had crawled up the drain leading from the main drain at the back of the house to the bath room. We went immediately to the bath room, and, finding that the snake had not made his appearance inside, I stopped up the opening into the drain with a towel, and the convict orderly, who had gone round to the outer end of the drain, began pushing a long bamboo up it. This drove the snake to the upper end. The convict, then, with a pickaxe, loosened a brick from the covering of the drain close to the wall of the house, while I stirred up the bamboo rod. The convict then gently and by degrees removed the brick, and in an instant the snake emerged fully from the drain, raising its hood and hissing at us. It then retreated back to the drain, when the convict dexterously seized it by the tail, and, drawing it out, held it tight by the neck. The convict then teased the snake with his coarse flannel 'kumblie,' or blanket, and it struck at it several times with its fangs; when, with a sudden jerk, the convict drew out the fangs in the blanket, and the snake became perfectly harmless.

"The snake was afterwards sent on board H.M. surveying schooner *Saracen*, and getting loose on board was summarily destroyed, for none on board had been told that its fangs had been removed."

The Crocodile.—Govindhoo, a convict employed at the Pulo Obin stone quarries, was admitted into hospital with a lacerated leg, the foot being almost severed from the body. He was visited by one of us, and told his story as follows:—

"I was walking along the sea beach close to the water, when I was suddenly seized from behind, and I at once saw that I was in the jaws of a crocodile. I had nothing in my hand but my 'roomāl,' or handkerchief, with my keys tied in one corner. I hit at his head with this, but it was of no use, and finding myself being dragged into deeper water, I suddenly thought I could dig out both his eyes, and I did it, and very shortly afterwards he let me go, and I half swam, half paddled back to the shore."

The convict's leg had to be amputated.

The Malays say that there are three descriptions of crocodiles, or, as they call them, "buaya." The first is the "katak" or frog crocodile, the second the "labu" or gourd crocodile, and the third is the "tumbaga" or copper crocodile. The frog crocodile is the most active, and we have often been told by Malay boatmen, when going up a river, to keep our hands and shoulders well within the boat, for fear of their sudden attack. There are, however, known to our naturalists a dozen or more different forms of the crocodile proper, and it is said that they have been found up to thirty feet in length; but from eighteen feet to twenty feet is the longest found in the Straits of Malacca. They may often be seen in the Malay rivers, and on the coast, floating in the water, with the snout well above the surface, on the look out for prey.

*   *   *   *   *

No. 7

The Chinese have one superstition amongst many in regard to tigers. They believe that when a person is killed by a tiger his "hantu," or ghost, becomes the slave of the beast and attends upon it; that the spirit acts the part of a jackal, as it were, and leads the tiger to his prey; and so thoroughly subservient does the ghost become to his tigerish master, that he not infrequently brings the tiger to the presence of his wife and family, and calmly sees them devoured before his ghostly face.

A very ingenious tiger trap was invented by Mr. Frank Shaw, of Caledonia sugar estate, in Province Wellesley, which is worth describing. It was constructed at the foot of a small hill, about a mile away from the estate, where there was a considerable area of secondary jungle and gigantic bracken fern, a favourite resort of tigers. A trench, about four or five feet wide, was opened in the sloping ground for a distance of ten or twelve feet; stout stakes were driven in the trench close to the sides, projecting some three or four feet above the ground, for about two-thirds the length of the trench; the remaining one-third at the upper end was converted into a strong cage, or pen. This pen communicated with the other part of the trench by an opening in which a gate in two flaps was fitted; a heavy cover, weighing ten or twelve cwt, of round logs was made to fit the open part of the trench, and so arranged in an inclined position, and connected by triggers with the two flaps, that any attempt to open the latter released the upper end of the heavy cover and allowed it to fall down in the trench. A couple of goats were tied at the far end of the pen as a bait, and were kept there constantly, food being taken to them by a convict coolie. After the trap had been set for some time, the coolie who fed the goats came running to the house one day with the news that a tiger was caught in the trap. Of course every one set out immediately to secure the animal. The tiger had evidently tried to push in between the two flaps to get at the goats: this released the triggers, and the jerk and movement of the cover had evidently alarmed the animal, who tried to back out; but the weight and force of the falling cover on its back had pressed the beast down flat on the ground and rendered him powerless. The difficulty now was to dispatch the tiger. Only its hind quarters could be seen; and a revolver shot was fired into the body. After a while the cover was raised a little, and a bullet in the brain finished the work. The cover was then entirely removed, and the carcase taken out of the trap; the fore and hind feet were tied together, and it was slung on a pole in the usual way, eight Kling convict coolies lifted the load and started for the sugar mills. They, however, soon got tired. Half a dozen more convicts, who were at work on the road, were then called in to assist, and at last they reached their journey's end.

On arrival at the sugar mills it was skinned, the skin becoming the property of the manager, and the natives disposed of the flesh. The animal proved to be a tigress, and evidently had young cubs, as she had a quantity of milk. This the Chinese coolies were very eager to secure, as it is by them considered to be a valuable medicine. We never heard whether any more tigers were caught in this trap.

The ordinary method, however, adopted for catching tigers is by means of pits, which are dug from twelve to fifteen feet in depth, and somewhat pyramidal in form. Sometimes pointed stakes are fixed in the bottom of the pit. The mouth is covered over with light brushwood, and when convenient, a tree is felled and laid a few feet from it across the tiger's track, so that the animal in leaping off the tree adds impetus to his own weight in falling into the trap.

The trouble of digging these pits is not so slight as might be supposed, as the construction of a pit in the proper manner fully occupies a couple of convicts a fortnight, besides the risk of being interrupted in their labour by the tiger happening to encounter them, and, naturally enough, on finding the work they were engaged upon, testifying his displeasure at the treachery they were meditating against him by making a meal of them.

An Indian sportsman wrote to the *Singapore Free Press*, at the time when so many Chinese were being destroyed at Singapore, saying:—

"I have been accustomed to tiger hunting in India, but the same mode could not be adopted here, the jungle being of a different character. Indeed, the only plan which is likely to be attended with success is by setting traps; and it is to be regretted that the local Government did not long since take some pains to prove this to the cultivators. Had this been done, many lives might have been spared." The Chinese were evidently delighted at the interest shown by the European gentlemen on the last occasion, and it is to be hoped that they will exert themselves to rid the island of tigers by this means.

While the ravages of tigers were destructive of human life on land, crocodiles were almost equally as mischievous on the coast and in the rivers, and many Chinese and other natives fell a prey to their voracity. Sometimes bathers were attacked; at other times fishermen, shrimp catchers, and oyster divers were carried off or attacked by them. Some crocodiles, like some tigers, have a peculiar partiality to human flesh, and often display remarkable ingenuity in gratifying their appetites. Regular man-eater crocodiles existed in some of the rivers in the Straits Settlements, notably in the rivers in Province Wellesley; but many were found also in the rivers in Singapore and Malacca, as well as on the sea coast. Some of these man-eaters were very bold, and would attack natives in their canoes, sometimes getting under the canoe and upsetting it in order to devour the occupants. Cases have been known of persons being snatched out of boats. A case of this kind happened in the Prye River, in Province Wellesley. The supervisor in charge of the public works was proceeding in a ferry boat with some convicts to repair the boundary pillar, situated some distance up the river, when suddenly a splash was heard, and his convict orderly, who was squatting in the bow of the sampan, or boat, uttering a cry, stood up, at the same time pointing to the stern of the boat. Upon looking round, a Chinaman, who had been seated in the stern of the boat, was found to be missing. A crocodile had, as it were, shot up out of the water, and, seizing the Chinaman by the waist, had drawn him down into the river, and nothing more was seen of them at the time. Shortly afterwards, a canoe with a Malay man and his wife in it was upset near the same spot by a crocodile, and both of them disappeared. A little later a Kling, who had been in the habit of diving for mud oysters near Qualla Prye Ferry for many years, and had repeatedly been cautioned about his danger in doing so, was missed, and it was ascertained that he had been seen diving for oysters as usual, and had suddenly disappeared, and had not been seen to come up again.

This sort of thing went on for some time, and the crocodiles could not be caught. At last the convicts stationed at Prye town convict lines succeeded in capturing a large crocodile, and this is how they managed it. They prepared a bait by tying a strong hook underneath the body of a pariah dog. One end of a piece of light iron chain was fastened to this hook; the other end was fastened to a log of very light wood as a buoy. They then went in a boat to that part of the river where the greater number of casualties had occurred. Here they drifted about, at the same time pinching the dog's ears and otherwise tormenting him to make him yelp. After watching the surface of the water for some time, they descried the V mark on the water indicating the approach of a crocodile; then, throwing the dog and buoy overboard, they pulled away for some distance to watch the result.. They saw the crocodile rapidly approaching the dog, who was swimming for his life. Suddenly there was a howl, and the dog disappeared. Then they watched the buoy, which would sometimes disappear under the water and then rise again to the surface; and in this manner they traced the crocodile, and followed him into a small creek, where he crawled on shore; and there they dispatched him with musket balls. This crocodile measured fourteen feet from the tip of his nose to the end of his tail, and was said to be the largest specimen captured at that time, but they have been known to reach from eighteen to twenty feet in length. Upon opening him a human leg and a pair of Chinaman's trousers were discovered, and it was concluded that this was one of the man-eaters.

As an illustration of the effect of shock upon the human system at the sight of wild beasts, we may mention a case of a Malay fisherman who was shrimping on the bar at the mouth of the Krian River (Province Wellesley), when a crocodile approached him from behind and seized him by the thigh. The Malay drew his parang and hacked away at the creature's nose until he let go. Some convicts stationed at Nebong Tubal and a Malay police peon saw what was happening and put off in a boat to his assistance. They rescued the poor fellow, and the police conveyed him at once by boat to the hospital at Butterworth, where his wounds, which were not very serious, were attended to; but the shock to the nervous system was so great that the man lost his reason, and would constantly leave his cot and walk down the hospital ward, moving his hands up and down, as if in the act of shrimping. He died shortly after. A similar case of shock, and a well-known story in the Straits Settlements, occurred in Province Wellesley, but this was from a tiger. A Roman Catholic priest was returning to his house after breakfasting with a planter at Alma, and when passing through some tall "lalang" grass a tiger suddenly sprang out into the path a few yards in front of him. The priest, with great presence of mind, suddenly opened his Chinese umbrella in the face of the tiger; the animal gave a leap round to one side, and the priest repeated the umbrella movement. The tiger then gave another leap round to the other side, and the umbrella action was again performed. This was renewed till the tiger, who evidently was not hungry, and had taken alarm, made a disappointed growl and bounded away into the high lalang grass, and the priest hastened on his way home. On reaching his house he took a cold bath, to brace up his nerves as he said; but the next day he was confined to his bed, and died a fortnight after the event, due entirely, it was said, to the shock that he had sustained.

No. 8

As we have already intimated, the house of correction at Singapore was under the management and control of the Convict Department; and there were frequently from thirty to forty Europeans confined in this prison, chiefly seamen on short sentences for neglect of duty on board ship.

When Sir Robert McClure was commanding a vessel of war in Chinese waters about 1859, his ship was on the Singapore station for some little time; and upon his arrival he sent in to the house of correction a very incorrigible man-of-war's man named John —— (we will not give his surname, for he may be yet alive). This man had been several times punished while the ship was in China, and had been twice sentenced to be flogged. We heard all about him from the officer of the ship who had brought him ashore.

His sentence was three weeks' imprisonment: the first week in solitary confinement on bread and water, and congee or rice gruel diet. Upon his receipt into the prison, after the usual routine, he was placed in one of the penal cells, and bread and water set before him. Before the cell door was closed, he looked hard at the chief warder, saying, "Take away that filth; I won't eat it." The chief warder reported to the Superintendent that the man in the cells was a dangerous-looking character, and he was afraid we should have trouble with him, for he had never seen a man with such a hang-dog look. The morning of the second day he had touched neither bread nor water, though fresh had been given him, and in a churlish manner he said to the chief warder, who had remonstrated with him, "I'll eat the tail of my shirt first, before I eat what you bring me." The doctor visited him, and made his report to the Superintendent that he was a strong man, and in excellent health, and that he might be safely left until hunger obliged him to eat, but that he would see him twice a day.

Upon the afternoon of the second day the Superintendent himself, upon his inspecting the prisoners in the penal cells, entered this prisoner's cell, and the following dialogue ensued: "What is your name?" "What is that to you?" "But I am the Superintendent of this jail, and I ask you a simple question, and I want a simple answer." Then looking at the Superintendent with a disrespectful air the prisoner said, "Look at my warrant if you want to know it." "But I want to hear it from yourself." "Well, if it is any satisfaction to you, my name is John ——" The Superintendent then said, "Now I want to know what part of England you come from." "Well, what do you want to know that for? but I say again, if it is any satisfaction to you, I come from Saltash." "So you are a Cornishman, are you?" replied the Superintendent. "I know Saltash very well. It is a fine old place. And I know the Viaduct, and the cottages over against it. I wonder if you were born there in one of those cottages? Perhaps you were, and have a mother now living there; and if you have, and she knew that her son was now in an Indian jail, you would break that old woman's heart, that you would." This ended the conversation, and the cell door was shut.

Late in the evening the chief warder sent a special messenger to the Superintendent's quarters, asking him to visit the prison before nightfall, for the prisoner in the cells from the man-of-war in the harbour had something to communicate. So before it was yet very dark the Superintendent went down, and the cell door being opened, and the bull's-eye lantern turned upon the man, the Superintendent at once noticed a change in the countenance of his prisoner, for the reckless, devil-may-care expression had shifted, and as if by some good influence within. "Well, you sent for me, and I have come; what do you want?" said the Superintendent. Then in a faltering voice, and with tears in his eyes, the prisoner said, "I only want to say, sir, before I go to sleep, that you are the first man that has ever overcome me, for you spoke to me of my 'mother'; and now, sir, you can do anything you like with me, and I'll carry out my sentence properly, and go back aboard my ship and do my duty as a British sailor ought to do."

And he did; and after his release went in the ship on to Bombay, from whence the Superintendent heard from Sir Robert McClure that John ——— was as well behaved a man as he had on board, and that the treatment he had received in the Singapore jail had quite altered his nature, and he would like to know the prescription for it.

Very often, when a long course of positive punishment has ceased to have its effect, a contrary treatment may lead to quite a change in the character, and if anything will touch the heart of a vicious Briton, it is to bring him to think upon the early counsels of a godly mother.

Footnotes:

Major McNair.

Literally gouged the animal.

Shreds of tough rope are better.

H.M.S. Esk.

Chapter XI

ABOLITION OF THE CONVICT DEPARTMENT AND DISPOSAL OF THE CONVICTS

On the separation of the Straits Settlements from British India in 1867, it was arranged that the Indian life convicts at Singapore should be transferred to Port Blair in the Andaman Islands. In the course of correspondence which took place on the subject, His Excellency the Governor of the Straits Settlements proposed, in respect of those convicts who were to continue in the Straits, that a liberal use of the power of pardon should be made in the case of such convicts, the nature of whose crimes and whose subsequent character warranted it.

The Government of India agreed to this proposal, with the proviso that pardon should be conditional on convicts not returning to India, or in the case of Burmese to Burmah, without the special sanction in each case of the Government of India; and that this sanction would not be given in any cases in which the crime was "Thuggee" or "Dacoity," or robbery by administering poisonous drugs, or other form of organized crime, or in the case of mutiny or rebellion accompanied with murder.

Accordingly, the Straits Government authorities submitted lists of convicts whom they recommended for pardon. After consulting the local governments concerned, the Government of India issued orders in each case, authorizing the release and return to India of some of the convicts, granting conditional pardon to others, and refusing release on any account to the remainder.

This decision did not commend itself to the Straits Government, and His Excellency the Governor suggested the deputation of a special officer from India to inquire into the matter.

Mr. Brodhurst, of the Bengal Civil Service, was accordingly deputed. This officer extended his inquiries to the cases of other convicts brought specially to his notice by the Straits Government; and on receipt of his report, the Government of India granted unconditional releases in certain cases, while in others the convicts were pardoned conditionally on their not leaving the Straits.

On this representation by the Straits Government, His Excellency the Governor-General in Council, having reconsidered the subject, decided that any Indian or Burmese, who had completed twenty-five years' imprisonment and bore a good character, should be released, with permission to return to India or Burmah, provided he, or she, as the case might be, was not convicted of one of the offences enumerated below, viz.:—

1. Thuggee.

2. Dacoity.

3. Professional poisoning.

4. Belonging to a gang of Dacoits.

5. Belonging to a gang of Thugs.

6. Mutiny or rebellion with murder.

Of those who did not come under this category, some were pardoned unconditionally; others were released after they had completed twenty-five years' imprisonment, on condition that their conduct continued satisfactory. Of those who were pardoned unconditionally many returned to their own country; but when they arrived there they found things so uncongenial that they returned to the Straits and settled down as shopkeepers, cowkeepers, cartmen, etc., and most of them sought and obtained employment either with private individuals or in the Public Works Department. Several of the skilled artificers, who had been petty officers, were employed as sub-assistant overseers and gangers on public works, where their services proved to be of great utility, their prison training having rendered them much more to be relied upon than free men, and, as far as we have been able to ascertain, none of them have been reconvicted.

Of the total number of convicts in the Straits at the time when the convict establishment was broken up in 1873—

256	had been transported for				Thuggee.
581	"	"	"	"	Dacoity.
21	"	"	"	"	Professional poisoning.

" " " "	Robbery with murder, including highway robbery and gang robbery.
269	

1,127

The remainder were nearly all for murder, for being accomplices in murder, or for robbery with violence, and for felony.

Chapter XII

DISEASES AND MALINGERING

Perhaps a few observations on the principal diseases to which these Indian convicts were liable may be found useful; and we take for the purpose the statistics of the year 1863-64 as given in Appendix No. 2, when nostalgia did not occur. In alluding to these diseases, we shall at the same time notice the locality of the Singapore jail, and the composition of the soil on which it was built. It is now universally recognised that the soil on which communities reside continuously does in a measure influence their health.

So many works on hygiene have, however, been written, and so much has been said by medical experts on this subject, that we may almost say that it has been exhaustively treated. What we wish to show is simply that soil and locality do not influence all communities alike.

The site of the Singapore jail in Brass Basa Road was originally a piece of low ground saturated with brackish water; and the convicts themselves were, as we have elsewhere stated, employed in conveying red earth from the side of Government Hill to reclaim most of this marsh, in order to erect thereon the necessary buildings for their occupation. The site had to be raised from two to four feet, and the red earth was what might be called disintegrated laterite or clay ironstone. When the finished level was completed, it was about two feet above high water mark S.T. The surface of the enclosure had been so thoroughly trodden down, rolled, and graded to the drains and into the adjoining canal, that, with the periodical coatings of pure white sand from the Serangoon sand pits that had been laid over it, it had become almost impervious to water; and this we would notice particularly, for it had much to do with the sanitary condition of the jail and its inmates.

The dormitories were further raised slightly over two feet above the general surface, and their floors were carefully laid, so as literally to be as dry as a bone.

From Appendix No. 2 it will be seen that the principal disease from which these Indian convicts suffered was "fever," but not of a dangerous type; for, upon comparing the admissions to hospital with the deaths from this disease in all three settlements during the year referred to, we find that in Singapore and Penang they were *nil*, and but seven in Malacca. The next ailment which presented numerous cases were abscesses and ulcers, and the deaths from this cause amounted only to one in Singapore. Many of these ulcers were on the legs, and were caused by grit getting between the skin and the leather band worn under the fetter rings of convicts in the fourth and fifth classes. Stomach and bowel complaints rank next on the list, but we find that the deaths here only amounted to units. Rheumatic affections were numerous, caused perhaps in that damp climate from working on extra-mural duties and returning to jail in wet clothes with the wind blowing on them. A few cases of dropsy appear on the list, the largest number occurring in Penang, three only at Singapore. There were ordinary cases of œdema.

The death-rate to strength per cent, from ordinary diseases for the year given was 2.20 for Singapore, 3.82 for Penang, and 3.17 for Malacca. Perhaps the special attention to sanitation in Singapore may account for the death-rate being lower here than at the sister settlements.

After the convict jail had been broken up, and the convicts had all left it, the jail was handed over to the prison authorities to be converted into a criminal prison for the whole settlements. Not long after this change had taken place a very peculiar disease broke out amongst the inmates. It was known as Beri-beri, or, as some call it, the "Bad sickness of Ceylon." It is a very serious disease, and some think it arises from extreme exertion without sufficient sustenance to the body. In 1878 the ratio of mortality in the prison had risen to 16.20 per cent.; in 1879 it was further augmented to 20.63 per cent. The Local Government deemed it necessary without delay to appoint a Committee of Inquiry into the possible causes which had given rise to the spread of this disease. The conclusion at which they arrived was that it was due to the want of proper drainage of the site, so that the soil had got water-logged, and had generated malaria; also, that the prisoners needed a more nitrogenous diet. They advised the erection of an entirely new prison on a better and more elevated locality. These suggestions were all adopted, and the Committee in their judgment were greatly aided by Dr. Irvine Rowell, C.M.G., the Principal Civil Medical Officer, who formed one of the Committee.

There was no time lost by the Government with the Colonial Engineer (Major McNair) in preparing plans and erecting on the west side of Pearl's Hill, near the old civil jail, a prison on the cellular system, and after the most approved English model; but the change of site did not effectually remove the disease, for as late as the year 1884 "there were 262 cases under treatment. In the first nine months of that year the deaths were comparatively small, but during the latter three months they increased, constituting nearly one half of the total deaths during that period." Dr. Kerr attributed this increase to exacerbation in the type, and epidemicity of the disease.

It is not necessary, nor is it within our province, to attempt a description in detail of this disease; and happily it is mostly confined to Ceylon and the Malay Archipelago, though it occurs occasionally in China and Japan, where in the former country it is known as "Tseng," and in the latter as "Kak-ki." It is referred to in a book we have quoted in the body of this work, viz., that written by "Godinho de Eredia" in 1613, reproduced by M. Leon Janssen in 1882. It is called there bere-bere, which in the Malay language signifies a "sheep," or a "bird which buries its eggs in the sand," and is not now known by the Malays under that name, as far as we can gather, as a "disease." Godinho de Eredia says that the Malays cured it by the use of a wine made from the nipa palm, from whence we know a saccharine fermentable juice exudes from the cut spadices of this and other species. They call this juice "tuaca." Marco Polo alludes to the same wine in his second book, chapter xxv.

Some authorities say it arises from malarious exhalations, favoured by damp, or over-crowding in buildings improperly ventilated. To this latter cause we are inclined to attribute the outbreak in the Singapore prison; for when the prison was occupied by the Indian convicts, the area of open space round the different wards and buildings was well exposed to the action of sun and wind, but after its conversion into a criminal prison, this open space was divided off by high division walls, and for the purpose of shot drill and work sheds the enclosure was still further crowded. Perhaps the disturbance also of the soil may have had something to do with it, for we have known instances in the town where the excavation of subsoils had liberated noxious gases.

It was, however, very remarkable that during the period of over twenty-five years when this jail was occupied by the Indian convicts, not a single case of beri-beri was known to have occurred. The medical officers were quite unable to account for this, and of its non-occurrence in other parts of the town.

The Rev. Wallace Taylor, M.D., of Osaka in Japan, attributed the disease to a microscopic spore found largely developed in rice, and which he had also detected in the earth of certain alluvial and damp localities.

FEIGNED DISEASES

The question of feigned diseases should find a place in a work treating upon convicts, for amongst a number of natives in confinement—and indeed also amongst European prisoners where—regular work is insisted upon, and idleness in any is severely punished, it is but natural that some should be found to resort to expedients to escape work, or, in other words, to malinger.

Perhaps the most frequent cases of convicts in irons was the encouraging of sores round the ankles, where the iron rings of their fetters were placed; and this was done, notwithstanding the precaution always taken to guard the ankles with leathern bands for the rings to rest upon. When suspicion was attached to a convict in irons that he was tampering with his leg sores, he was at once detailed to work with the gang beating out coir from cocoanut husks: it involved no use of the legs, but it was the hardest of labours. The result was that the convict soon gave up the trick, and begged to return to outdoor work with his own gang. Of course there were cases where convicts working on roads or at sand pits may get grit below their leathers, which, without knowing it at the time, would cause a sore; but such cases were readily distinguished from those sores wilfully caused and designedly kept open.

We had no cases of feigned insanity or any species of mania, but cases of imitated "moon blindness," or dim-sightedness, did occur now and again for the purpose of shirking night watch.

Upon one occasion we had a remarkable instance of shamming blind, which is worth giving in detail. The case was that of a life convict transported from Madras, who complained that lime had suddenly got into both of his eyes while employed at the lime kilns. It was deemed by the medical authorities as not unnatural that he should become blind from caustic quick-lime, and he was admitted into the convalescent gang, where he had only the simple and easy task of picking oakum. The deceit was as cleverly kept up for years as it was cleverly commenced at the outset, and was only detected by Dr. Cowpar, a hard-headed Scotchman and skilful surgeon, who, during the absence of the permanent incumbent, had been appointed by the Government to officiate as medical officer of the jail. After his inspection of the invalids in the convalescent gang, he looked at the eyes of the "blind man"; and, having some suspicion in his mind, he decided that he should be put aside for closer examination. When the inspection was over, the "blind man" was taken, and carefully led by the peon in charge of the gang to one of the long wards, when he was told to walk up and down in the presence of the doctor. After he had made two or three trips, the doctor directed two men to hold a long pole about a foot off the ground on the track he had to pass. When he came to the pole he fell over it flat on his face, and to the bystanders it seemed rather an inhuman proceeding on the part of the doctor, but he had observed an ominous pause before the convict had struck the pole with his legs.

He sent for his case of instruments, and, withdrawing a probe, he with little difficulty removed the film off both of the man's eyes, which proved to be nothing more nor less than the thin membrane found inside an egg, which the convict had artfully introduced, and renewed from time to time. Of course he was reduced to the fifth class, and to the hardest labour.

We have often thought it strange that none of his fellow-convicts appeared to suspect him, or if they did, they kept it back from the jail authorities; and certainly to any casual observer the deception was complete, and it was the best case of feigned blindness we have ever known or heard of.

Upon the whole, however, cases of malingering were few and far between, as most of the convicts became after a time interested in the works upon which they were engaged, and those in irons were ever on the look-out for promotion to a higher class. Sometimes there was a case of feigned rheumatism or paralysis, but the application of the galvanic battery invariably cured them of that after a few powerful shocks.

Chapter XIII

CONCLUSION

We have now given a full, and, as far as we could, a succinct account of the system pursued in the old Singapore jail. We have traced the history of the convict establishments in all the penal settlements in those seas, and have shown the progressive improvements in the convict prisons up to the time when, as was acknowledged by many competent authorities, a system of organization and discipline had been satisfactorily attained to, especially at the headquarter jail at Singapore. We have also shown the number and variety of industries that were from time to time introduced, and the utilization of trained artificers in the construction of important public works in the Straits Settlements.

Perhaps we may say that the conduct of these prisons from the year 1825, down to 1845, was in a measure experimental; but at any time we do not assert that the system was free from defects. But on the whole, in the treatment of these trans-marine convicts, it worked with remarkable success, and was well adapted to their condition and circumstances; for it must not be forgotten that we had to deal with convicts who in great part had expiated their crimes by a sentence of banishment to a foreign country, which we have already explained was more severely felt by a native of India than could possibly be by any European. As a matter of fact, owing to caste prejudices, transportation across the seas was to many of the Indian convicts worse than death itself, for it carried with it not only expulsion from caste, but, owing to their wrong conception of fate, or "nusseeb" as they call it, a dread of pain and anguish in another existence.

In the later management of this jail, to all fresh arrivals for life there was a period of probation of three years, during which time they were fettered and worked in gangs upon the public roads. This was thoroughly punitive, and with no liberty whatever. They were, in point of fact, full of fears and practically without hope. After a time, they began to find that the only chance of any amelioration from this hard labour was by a course of good conduct; and they saw before them their own countrymen, who had once been similarly circumstanced, occupying better positions and employed on less distasteful work. They also heard from their fellows that several had attained to a ticket of leave, and were earning for themselves an honest livelihood in the place of their banishment. This, then, was their encouragement; but not a few at first, however, though carefully treated in hospital, died from "nostalgia," or "love of country," before they could complete their term of probation.

The late General, then Captain Man, who, as we have already said, did a great deal in the consolidation of the convict system of Singapore, went from the Straits Settlements to the Andamans, and inaugurated there the same system; but we learn that since his time convicts upon first arrival from India are placed for a certain period in separate cells, and no doubt the authorities had good and weighty reasons for the change. We have no report as to the advantage or otherwise of this probationary alteration, but from what we have said, it will be seen that we incline to the belief that for this class of native convicts work in irons upon the public roads is a better "first trial" than to place them under what is known to us as the "cellular system."

For local prisoners, who after their sentences have expired are returned to the town, we do advocate the "cellular system," and have ourselves designed and built for term convicts several wards upon this system. The advantage gained is complete isolation from one another for a fixed period, and the indiscriminate admixture of classes thus avoided, and so possibly by this means a recrudescence of crime in the place prevented; but with convicts under banishment, and mostly for a life term, we think the conditions are very different, and we prefer the plan adopted in the old Singapore convict jail.

The punishments in force by our laws are of course designed to deal out retributive justice to the prisoner for his offence against society, and so to prevent, if possible, a repetition of the offence by others, and by this means to protect society against evil-doers. There is no wish to punish with any vindictive feeling, but rather, if it can be done, to bring about the reform of the prisoner, and to take away from him the desire to offend again; and as "Beccaria," the Italian philanthropist, well said, "those penalties are least likely to be productive of good effect which are more severe than is necessary to deter others."

In the later days of our Singapore convict jail, of which time only are we in a position to express an opinion, the treatment of the convicts was one of discipline from beginning to end. There was first the probationary period under fetters, in gangs upon the public roads, or upon the severest hard labour; next the period of freedom from this restraint and a time of test, and if they stood this test well, then advancement to a position of trust, either on the lower rung of the prison warder-staff, with a belt of authority across the shoulder, or, if an aptitude for any trade was evinced, to the position of a novice in the workyard, at whatever branch of industry the convict was thought to be best suited. There was then open to the prison warder a rise in grade to that of peon, with a distinctive badge, and eventually to the highest grade of a tindal or duffadar, if duly qualified. In the case of the industrial class there was also open a promotion to a higher grade, and eventually to that of a foreman of artificers. All were fully occupied and employed, and the jail was in point of fact a busy hive of industry, the pervading idea of the convict authorities being to teach the convict to love labour, and to take a personal interest in it.

We know that there are still some who think that no prisoner, while undergoing his sentence, should be allowed to feel any pleasure in the occupation in which he may be engaged; and hence they advocate the crank, shot drill, and other aimless tasks, which serve but to irritate, and do not the least good to the heart, from whence all our actions spring. For a short term of probation, no doubt, the task should be irksome; but when this is over and it should not be prolonged work should be given which would tend to call out the best feelings, restore self-respect, and act as a sort of cordial to remove lowering and depression. To explain by a homely instance what we mean, we will mention an incident that occurred to one of us when building the Woking prison in 1866. A convict undergoing sentence there, of the labouring class, was found to be of an exceptionally dogged and dull nature. Nothing pleased him; he was disgusted with the world, and wished he was out of it. After a time he was tried at plain brick-laying in a foundation, and gradually began to handle a brick rather well. He seemed to grow step by step more reconciled to his lot, and was advanced to work upon a chimney-piece. A day or two later he was asked how he was getting on. He then replied, with a bright smile upon his face, "Oh, very well, sir, now! I likes my chimbley-piece, and dreams of her at nights in my lonely cell."

Hence we see how the implacable temper of this convict gave way over a congenial bit of work, and the first step was thus taken towards his reformation of character, and he continued to improve until his release from prison.

Herbert Spencer says with truth, "that experience and experiments have shown all over the world that the most successful criminal discipline is a discipline of decreased restraints and increased self dependence"; and to a degree of this "self dependence" the convict we refer to had been encouraged to aspire.

Of course, in all criminal prisons we must expect a certain percentage of incorrigible characters, who under the best training cannot be brought under control; but the bulk of those in the old Singapore jail, and we had often as many as two thousand at a time, were well behaved, and gave evidence of the good influence of a course of discipline upon them; for when they were advanced to a ticket-of-leave, and thrown again on their own resources, they very rarely a second time came under the cognisance of the police, but peaceably merged into the population, and earned their livelihood by honest means.

We have one word to say in reference to the employment of these convicts as warders over their fellow-prisoners; a system, so far as we are aware, then unattempted either in Europe or America, even in a modified form. We do not, however, see why, in the case of well-behaved and suitable European convicts sentenced to long periods of penal servitude, some might not be placed in certain such positions of trust under free warders; and as the new prison rules for our jails may possibly involve a large increase in the warder staff, it has occurred to us that the system might have a trial to a limited extent; but we are, of course, not in a position to speak with any authority upon the subject as affecting our own prisons. In our case, with the exception of two or three European warders, the whole warder staff were convicts; and at first, certainly, there was the fear that so large a number of convict warders might side with the convicts, when a rule they might have thought repugnant to all, was introduced by the governing body. There also appeared the danger that discipline might be undermined by a system of favouritism, especially amongst men of the same caste, or that they would shut their eyes to breaches of the rules.

None of these apprehensions were, however, experienced; but, on the contrary, these convict warders were always the first to apprise the authorities of any contemplated attempt at escape, or of any ill-feeling that might be brewing amongst any particular class, or breach of prison rules; so that, in a great measure, they acted in the double capacity of both detectives and police. It was only upon very rare occasions that a convict warder had to be disrated; and the punishment amongst them consisted for the most part in fines for want of vigilance and attention to detail, and such like petty offences. They all manifested the highest appreciation of the trust reposed in them, and lived in a perpetual fear that they might forfeit their position, and have to begin anew the whole course of jail punishment.

It need scarcely be said that great care was exercised to single out men of the best character, and to the highest posts those who could take upon themselves responsibility as men of purpose and discretion. Promotion in the different grades was made only by the Superintendent, who in our case was an officer who had served in India, knew natives of most sects and races, and was acquainted with their habits and customs, and spoke one or two of their languages.

The prison system in all its branches worked in perfect harmony, and all the parts of it seemed to be adapted to each other. Discipline was maintained throughout, and the artificer gang, as we have shown, developed a high skill in their various trades; so that important public works could be executed without difficulty or embarrassment. Those also who had passed through its course, and were admitted back to society upon a ticket of leave, as a rule behaved themselves as good citizens.

In the extraction of labour from the convicts, there was no desire on the part of the Government to work the establishment with a view to show any pecuniary profit in the returns; though, as it proved, the actual cost to the State was often more than reimbursed by their labour, estimated as it was at two-thirds of that prevailing in the place, and the material at half the market price. However, in regard to this part of the question we might here quote "Jeremy Bentham," who once wisely said of prison labour, "It is not the less reforming for being profitable."

We would now take leave of our old Singapore jail, as indeed, owing to the result of the earnest entreaty of the community to the Government, it finally took leave of us in 1873, though in our judgment perhaps a little too prematurely in the best interests of the colony.

We can only hope that in the record we have now given, we have furnished some suggestions for general application to those who, like ourselves, are concerned not merely with the punishment of the criminal, but also with his reformation, both as a question of social science, and to the prisoner's own ulterior benefit.

This reformation could, we think, be best brought about by a course of severe probationary discipline at the outset, to be followed up by continuous employment upon productive occupations and trades, so as to encourage within the criminal a lively diligence and a persevering industry; ourselves meanwhile also encouraged in the task by the words of Shakespeare, that

"There is some soul of goodness in things evil,Would men observingly distil it out."*King Henry V.*, Act. iv., Scene i.

Milton Keynes UK
Ingram Content Group UK Ltd.
UKHW040816051024
449151UK00004B/270

9 789362 519979